"The combination of a recessionary economy and ... ...rated advancement of technology has caused a tipping point in the way executives are found and hired. There hasn't been a better "how-to" book published that speaks to the executive about the competitive employment landscape and how to navigate it using today's digital presence platforms. This is a must read... and not just for the unemployed! "

--Brian Vincent, Founder, CORPORATE TRIAGE, LLC

" ... incredibly practical and motivating. I've written more defining and credibility-generating content since the seminar than in the last year."

--Jim Tinney, CTO

"Leadership hiring has entered a new paradigm and, if you are looking to compete, it is time to re-tool. This must-read guide is a roadmap to maintaining your competitiveness in the new world of executive career search."

--Ken Myer, former CEO, WTIA

"... Colleen has come out with a timely book that recognizes a fundamental transformation in the nature of senior level executive jobs which increasingly require you to continually demonstrate your value proposition. She is asking each executive to think about: what's my "business model" and core competency ? How should I market myself ? What tools are there for me to use ? Her book should prove to be an invaluable help to executives in the job market!

--Binay Sugla, Executive Chairman, Mobile Matrix Inc.

"... ahead of the curve in supporting the new job search dynamics that now include networking portals like Twitter, Facebook, LinkedIn and others."

--Robert Bachman, Director, Business Development

"This is a game-changer for anyone who has more than 10 years' work history and is looking to "crack the code" of standing out in the mass of active job candidates."

--Valerie Campbell CPA, Finance Manager

"As a business owner, I'm looking to hire problem-solvers that can address our immediate needs. Most candidates miss that point and focus on their own needs, likes and aspirations. Those candidates rarely get to interview with us. Read Colleen's book. She really gets it."

--Gary Scroggs, Partner, IS Domain, Inc.

"(Colleen) is on top of the online brand presence required in today's very competitive job market. Her job search seminar is highly recommended and definitely worth the time."

--Joe Herzog, Marketing Executive

From Bedlam to Boardroom

from
Bedlam to
Boardroom

How to get a derailed executive career back on track!

Colleen Aylward

ISBN-13: 978-1456597559
ISBN-10: 1456597558

Product or brand names used in this book may be trade names or trademarks. Where we believe that there may be proprietary claims to such trade names or trademarks, the name has been used with an initial capital or in its logo format. All such names have been used in an editorial manner without any intent to convey endorsement of or other affiliation with the name claimer. The author does not intend to express any judgment as to the validity or legal status of any such proprietary claims.

LinkedIn, the LinkedIn logo, the IN logo and InMail are registered trademarks or trademarks of LinkedIn Corporation and its affiliates in the United States and/or other countries.

This book is available through Amazon.com and other retailers

Book Cover Design by Symantry Marketing, LLC

DEDICATION

This book is dedicated to every business person who has recently been, or is about to be fired, laid off, shut out, made redundant, or squeezed out in this global economic bedlam.

CONTENTS

INTRODUCTION

CHAPTER 1 RESET

CHAPTER 2 DEFINE

PREFACE

From Bedlam to Boardroom is the definitive guide for executives who are navigating their way through the new job search landscape – many for the first time in their lives.

In meeting with hundreds of out-of-work executives in the past two years, I've too often witnessed the shock and confusion of those who were scorched by this financial recession not really knowing how to proceed. People like you.

In one of the most unstable times in U.S. history, when 15.2 million people are out of work, what is the answer to this hugely competitive quest for re-employment? Employers, faced with the uncertainties of the global economy and unknown implications of new national healthcare legislation, have frozen their hiring plans indefinitely. But sadly they are still barraged with hundreds of resumes from desperate job seekers.

Is this just a blip that will self-correct? When the economy comes roaring back, will the job search rules go back to what they once were? Will high-level generalists be back in demand? Will your next job come to you from your inner circle of business friends as usual? Will employers hire seasoned executives to oversee, critique, and evaluate others' work? Will your transferrable skills be meaningful to employers?

No. Things won't go back to those scenarios again. Moving forward in your career is all about *digitizing your brand* now.

- Positioning yourself on the global internet as an expert in something.
- Becoming an authority online.
- Solving particular problems in a particular niche and letting the world know that you did it and can do it again.
- Creating a virtual network of business connections as your audience and as your support infrastructure.
- And making sure that you are found.

But how do you do all this re-invention and positioning and digitizing of yourself? And when will you have time to do all of this? *And how will it get you a job?*

Drawing on 19 years in the retained search business from the employer side, my firm now offers succinct job search advice and critical visibility tools to our *candidate clients* through our Executive Job Search Program[1]. The contents of the program are reflected in these 170 pages that follow.

Starting with a straightforward slap-upside-the-head introduction to how things have changed, this rich resource gives much-needed advice and structured solutions for the employment road ahead.

Many chapters go into more detail than you might care to implement on your own. For you, the Executive Job Search Program may be the answer, because we go through these steps with you.

The point is that it's important for you to understand and embrace what the new employment landscape looks like for now and for the years ahead.

Things will never go back to the way they were. The world is an online community now, and the future of your employment status is highly dependent on your ability to adapt.

---

[1] Reference: the Devon James Executive Job Search Program ("Executive Program") which is described in the Epilogue of this book for those who are looking for more assistance. Or visit www.devonjames.com.

ACKNOWLEDGMENTS

Huge thanks to Liam Scanlan for his inspiration to forge ahead and write a book; to my dear friend Mary Luethe for reading it and reading it and reading it again; to my awesome SEO expert and reader, Lou Kertesz, for the gift of his non-judgmental support; to Loribeth Dalton for her constant validation of the message; to Robert Pinkerton for the cover, and the hours of work on the website in between his hospital visits; to my parents, James F. and Joyce Aylward for the much needed California hideout so this could be written, and for their constant encouragement as they tiptoed past my door; to Ashley Van Dyk for finding the time to read, edit, and comment while battling a month of New York snow storms; to Liz Tidyman for the generosity of her time, wordsmith expertise and detailed editing skills; to Randol Sargent for his invaluable inputs from an HR perspective; to JD Aylward for letting me "do what you gotta do" in the many hours I chose to write instead of hanging with him; and to the amazing Randy Brown, for the brilliant title and frequent cocktails, without which there might be no humor in these pages.

INTRODUCTION

THINGS HAVE CHANGED

"I'll be right back. I'm just going to run to the ATM machine and get $1000 for each of you who can write 400 words about your ONE specialty area by the time I get back."

This is what I tell the executive job seekers who attend my seminars. Their first reaction is:

"What the heck? I didn't come to this seminar to do homework... "

A split second later, the reaction becomes:

"....and anyway, I'm a C-level exec! I'm good at everything. I'm the orchestra conductor! I wave my hand and my minions do all that specialty stuff! I'm above all that in this stage of my career! I'm a true management generalist!"

For the last 100 years in the US, we have bred our fine American boys and girls to graduate college with the ideal of becoming the General Manager of some huge company, or Attorney General or yes, even the President of the United States. Anything less than that is a bit of a failure.

No? You don't think so? At the last cocktail party or golf game, were you OK with introducing yourself just as Bob Miller and not Bob Miller, CEO of CorpAmerica?

And the older you get, the more general and lofty you think your title should be: Chief of Everything Operational, for instance.

I saw a cocktail napkin once that said *"The older I get, the greater I was."*

Perception

Tell me if I'm wrong. At first glance, this graph describes you, right?

Consider Figure 0-1. The bigger the dots, the more masterful you are on a particular subject. And the more dots you have at that age means you have more subject areas in your knowledge base.

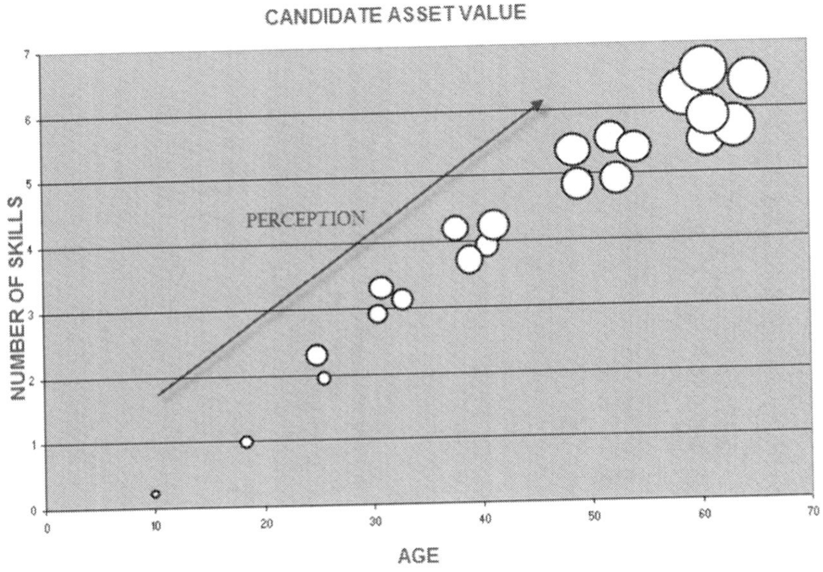

Figure 0-1

The PERCEPTION is that the older we get, the more things we master, until we are pretty much the master of everything by our 60s... or at least the master of a bunch of things that people ask us about in our daily jobs.

We know what we need to know. We know who to assign tasks to in order to accomplish a job. We have the industry contacts we need for partnerships and closing deals. We know all the terminology in our industry, all the vendors, and all the competitors and their products. We know the projections, the costs, the timelines in our business model, and all the dirty laundry of our management teams.

So this abundant knowledge is of huge asset value to our current employer. But what about the next one? What is our real "job market" value?

Reality

Let's look at Figure 0-2 and the typical accumulation and mastery of skills in a career.

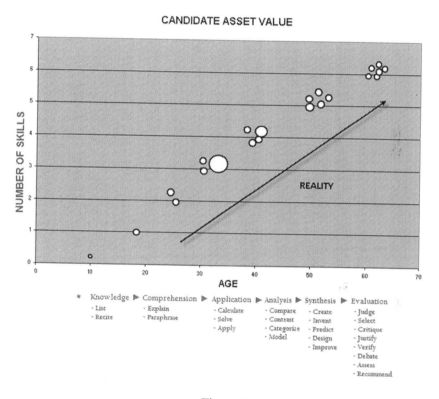

Figure 0-2

When we reach our late 20s, particularly if we've been to college, we start discovering a few things we're good at in the work world. Let's take a sales career as an example: We may find out we're fairly good at talking a customer through a tough problem over the phone, or delivering the perfect copy machine sales pitch.

Generally speaking, we're good at a set of skills because we have had good training. In our early 30s we might add a bit of management skills if we've been in charge of a few junior sales folks or a field support rep for the copy machines for instance. Our strongest skill, the stand-up sales pitch, remains our primary talent while we are working on improving our other skills by watching and learning from others.

By our late 30s and early 40s, we are combining our training and our experience to actually apply what we've learned. We are now solving problems with our own brains instead of just relying on the company guidelines.

In our 40s and 50s, we are using our Analysis and Synthesis talents to compare and model situations, predict outcomes, invent new solutions, etc.

But let's face it. By the time we're in our 50s, we've been following a trajectory set by our corporate structure, or we've been doing the same job at different companies. We're not learning new things at the same pace as in our 30s and 40s.

We are critiquing jobs that others do, and predicting where things might fail. We sit on boards and validate or debate others' opinions. We recommend courses of action for others to carry out.

So, in seeking the next job, here's the rub: the farther we get from the ground, the closer we are to the clouds and it gets pretty misty up there.

Our perception of being great at a lot of things is incorrect. Yes, we've had a lot of experiences that give us insight. Yes, we've done a lot of things over the years. But you don't really have those large dots at the top right corner of your chart. You have a bunch of small dots that acknowledge that you've touched a lot of things in the past.

Not to worry though. In this book, we start out right away in Chapter 1 with useful tips to help determine and state your biggest dots – your most marketable strengths – in a way that makes a difference to employers. And Chapter 2 will discuss the aggregation of all that data forming your asset value.

Who employers are hiring

Times have changed. Employers don't so much hire a title (CFO) anymore. Instead they hire problem solvers (e.g. "handled 2 mergers recently") who may happen to be given the title of CFO on the organizational chart.

And goodness knows there are problems out there to be solved.

Perch yourself on top of the Sears Tower and try to point to a company within a 2-mile visual radius that doesn't have at least one of the most common corporate problems *right now*:

- Failing subsidiary
- Diminishing morale
- Declining earnings
- Security of data
- Inventory shrinkage
- Lack of funding
- Financial duress
- Diversity inclusion
- Global competition
- Union issues
- Staying current with technology
- Scrambling to incorporate e-Marketing

These challenges all need immediate attention.

Today's employers are hiring, but they are not hiring executives who will take 6 months to get the lay of the land and learn the business. They are not hiring executives who "think it would be fun" or who "think it would be a next great challenge." Nor are they hiring execs with "transferable skills." And furthermore, they do not need "trouble shooters" who parachute in, tell them they have problems, and then leave.

Employers are hiring people who can solve their company's specific problems quickly – those who have solved the exact problem several times before in different companies and have proof of it.

These problems you've solved (and the keywords that you use to describe them) become important tools in positioning yourself to be found.

You'll learn more about this concept in Chapter 3.

And we'll talk in Chapters 6 and 7 about setting you up to be a known expert in these solution areas, which makes you an even more desirable candidate.

The truth about getting a job in today's market

"Just get me in front of the CEO!" says Josh Furman, one of my executive job search clients. Josh has been laid off from his lucrative Vice President position at a local high tech company and has no patience for learning the art of keyword populating or search engine scouring. He just wants to get in front of as many hiring authorities as possible.

Why? Because he is positive that he can talk his way into a job if he can just get the face-to-face interview.

Well there is a lot to say regarding this theory in today's hiring climate. Yes, it used to be true that executives could network their way onto the CEO's schedule – a golf foursome, a chance meeting at the local Starbuck's on Saturday, comp tickets to a Mariners game, a coincidental airport introduction – all schemes that used to work.

That was before CEOs were saddled with the long, iterative "best practices" for hiring that now include reams of due diligence, behavioral interviewing processes, corporate culture match screening, background checks, and all sorts of rules for the actual executive job interview that would take place after all candidates had been properly vetted.

So, as an out-of-work candidate seeking that immediate executive job interview in today's market, what are you considering as your strategy for doing this?

1. Keep trying the old ways to get in the chair across the desk from the CEO?
2. Seek out a recruiter who will market you into the CEOs?
3. Be proactive and provide the hiring team with all that "best practice" data they need upfront in order to qualify you for an executive job interview sooner?

Option 1 is simply an approach that is no longer effective in today's hiring market. With the oversight of Board Members and the slew of hiring guidelines and due diligence enforced by HR these days, it is not as easy to slide into a corporate job on a referral from a buddy or a shared box seat at the Clippers game.

Option 2 has its problems since professional recruiters don't market candidates to CEOs. They don't find jobs for people. They find people *for* jobs.

They make their money by obtaining a specific assignment from a company to fill a specific job within that company. The company pays the recruiter for presenting only the exact matches for that position. Therefore, YOU are not important to a recruiter unless you are an exact match to one of their current searches.

Having said that, on occasion, you will find a recruiter who offers to "market you" to employers, but beware of this. Many recruiters are just as desperate for "jobs" as you are. If a recruiter sends your resume to several companies hoping for some interest, and any of those companies has a policy *not* to pay recruiter fees, then you will be ignored for the next 6 months as a candidate for any position within that company – since your hiring would now cost them a headhunter fee.

IF you choose to use a recruiter, make sure they will only "market you" to companies with whom they have a written fee agreement. And even then, you'll have to consider that companies in this economy may prefer non-fee-bearing candidates.

Option 3 brings us to a definitive market advantage that executive candidates can *create for themselves*. (Recruiters won't do this for you. Career Counselors will do part of it for you. Outplacement centers will do a tiny piece of this for you.) So, yes I'm saying that it is now up to you to gather your data, polish it up, and position it where people will find you. That is one of the biggest shocks in the executive job seeker's world right now.

No more buddy network that will just move you into their company without question. No more putting the word out and getting scooped up the way you have always been before. No longer are you getting daily recruiting calls from Korn/Ferry, Heidrick & Struggles, or Egon Zehnder. They just don't have the volume of positions anymore.

Your choices are less and your chances are fewer, since there are now more executive-level job seekers on the market than there have been in 20 years. In this candidate-rich market, competition is tough enough for those few executive positions that become available. And internal HR and Recruiting departments are swamped with so many applications that the screening process becomes that much longer.

If you put yourself in the shoes of the hiring authority – shoes you may have worn yourself in the past – you'll realize that in this economy, what they want are heroes, saviors, "magic men" (and women!).

Confident and proven players. People who make a difference quickly. People with no baggage, no whining, no excuses. And for the next few years at least, it's an employer's market. They can and will be very selective. What they want is proof that you have solved their exact problems before in other companies.... several times.

Full disclosure

Another news flash. This is now a world of full disclosure. Upfront. No longer do you play cat and mouse in the courting process. No more "I'll give them the details once I get in front of them." First of all, you'll never get in front of them if you're not out there on the internet to be found.

83% of employers now use LinkedIn[2], Facebook, and Twitter to find new hires, according to a survey by recruiting platform Jobvite. Of those, by far the largest number, 89%, rely mainly on LinkedIn, followed by Facebook at 28% and Twitter at 14%.[3] This LinkedIn forum has over 100 million business members, so of course this is where recruiters and companies go *first* to look for people like you. In Chapter 4 we will go into more depth about LinkedIn.

Second, hiring companies want to know, and have ways to find out, *everything* about you before you go in. In fact, they are often directed to do heavy online due diligence on candidates before they even make the first shortlist. So you need to profile yourself as who you really are, what you do best, and who you know. And then you need to publish that profile where recruiters will find you. You need to create an online profile and "post it" on the internet in places that are most viewed by employers and recruiters. We will talk about this more in Chapter 3.

---

[2] LinkedIn (www.LinkedIn.com) is an online business network of over 100 million global members who share their connections, provide answers to questions and discuss industry topics. More about LinkedIn in Chapter 4.

[3] From Anne Fisher's blog at http://management.fortune.cnn.com/2011/01/13/10-ways-to-use-social-media-in-your-job-hunt/

Candidates who provide not only a resume, but links to their online profiles, their business networks, peer reviews, outside interests, philanthropy work, and evidence of solving specific business problems will be found faster, and be interviewed *before* those who have only a resume and/or no online profile to be found.

This is important. It's not an opinion. It's a fact.

How this book can help you

In the 10 chapters that follow, you may go through shock, despair, denial, stress, and come out the other end feeling overwhelmed.

OR, you may finish the book with a smile on your face, knowing that you are now armed with the tools you need to move forward quickly in your search for that next great executive position.

This book is a mini-version of the one-on-one Executive Job Search Program[4] (called "Executive Program" in this book). It's a starting point for those of you who have not yet embarked on the Executive Program but certainly need the strategy, tactics and tools addressed here. The end objective of the book *and* the program is to move you forward in getting connected quickly to career opportunities where you will be valued for your unique skills, paid accordingly, and seen as a perfect match to the company's culture and goals.

Let's begin.

---

[4] Reference: the Devon James Executive Program (which is described at the back of this book) for those who are looking for more assistance.

CHAPTER 1

RESET

The job search process has morphed while you were busy working.

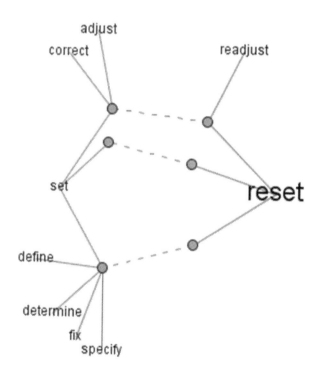

Your position in the universe

A frustrated Midwest executive wrote this recently in one of the online forums about his job search:

"[Recently], I was laid off for 8 months....

I look back at it now as how stupid I was in this economy to think that my outstanding resume and work experience would stand out in a crowd. For example, I once applied to a local position that I noticed on careerbuilder.com and the next day I followed up with a phone call to that company.

It took two days of persistent phone calls to finally talk to the owner of that company just to introduce myself and verify if the resume and cover letter was received. The owner simple [sic] told me that he just posted the job on CareerBuilder 3 days ago and he's already received 1500 resumes for one open position, and there's no way he'll be going through them all.

He told me that he's got a stack on his desk, the fax machine won't stop spitting them out and he will start at the top of the pile, find the first 3 candidates that match what he's looking for and then start the interview process, but he couldn't guarantee that he'd look at mine yet suggested I fax another one to him at his attention and maybe he'll look at it.

It's nuts out there and the market is so flooded by individuals applying for the same position that it's more of a lottery to even get someone to see your resume."

For every job opening today there are *at least* 100 applicants.

Applicants. I didn't say "qualified applicants." The percentage of qualified applicants for each job, however, is higher than it's been in over 20 years.

When I told this to Richard S., a former CEO in the aerospace industry, his response was "Well, maybe so for lower level jobs, but not at my level."

You may think this to be true but the fact is that in December 2010 there were nearly 2.5 million business and professional executives in the US who reported themselves as "unemployed."

As you and I both know, these numbers are low since many senior executives are:

a) too proud to be seen in the unemployment lines

b) suing their employer for severance instead of signing up for unemployment benefits

c) currently "under-employed" by helping colleagues or consulting until they can find that next high level job.

So the actual number of executives out on the market looking for the same job you are is much higher than reported by the BLS (Bureau of Labor Statistics). Conservatively then, there are at least 3 million executives looking for work in *all* salary ranges (read on to see why I use that number).

Your competitive statistics

Just to give you a feel for the number of people in your salary range, Figure 1-1 shows statistics about populations employed in some well-paid business and management occupations in 2009:

Occupational Employment Statistics survey by occupation, as of May 2009 for professional occupations with salaries between $92,000 and $220,000[5]		
Occupation	# of people Currently Employed in this occupation and salary range	Mean Annual Salary
Management occupations	**4,322,160**	
Chief executives	297,640	$167,280
General and operations managers	1,689,680	$110,550
Advertising and promotions managers	35,760	$97,670

[5] Bureau of Labor Statistics http://www.bls.gov/news.release/ocwage.t01.htm

Marketing managers	169,330	$120,070
Sales managers	328,980	$111,570
Public relations managers	53,270	$101,850
Computer and information systems managers	287,210	$120,640
Financial managers	495,180	$113,730
Human resources managers, all other	62,990	$105,510
Construction managers	204,760	$93,290
Education administrators, postsecondary	105,900	$95,340
Engineering managers	178,110	$122,810
Natural sciences managers	44,180	$127,000
Managers, all other	369,170	$99,100
Business and financial operations occupations	**408,240**	
Personal financial advisors	149,460	$94,180
Computer and information scientists, research	26,130	$105,370
Actuaries	17,940	$97,450
Mathematicians	2,770	$93,920
Aerospace engineers	70,570	$96,270
Computer hardware engineers	65,410	$101,410
Nuclear engineers	16,710	$100,350
Petroleum engineers	25,540	$119,960
Astronomers	1,240	$102,740
Physicists	13,630	$111,250
Economists	13,160	$96,320
Industrial-organizational psychologists	1,710	$102,570
Political scientists	3,970	$101,050

Figure 1-1

Add the desperate self-employed who aren't counted by the BLS and who are now looking for a paycheck. Plus a healthy number of "passive candidates" (those whom headhunters are actively pulling out of good jobs to place in other good jobs to make a fee). And finally, include the foreign candidates from other countries who are also qualified for those jobs.

So, potentially there are 5 - 7 million business executives in competition for management job openings in the US. The unsettling truth is that it is unknown how many executives in this salary range above are truly unemployed and competing with you. One million? Three million? The BLS counts household census data and employment security data, but the two don't match in the shifting sands of reporting, especially at this level of detail.

Remember the 100-applicants-per-job figure? How many do you think are your competitors for the few executive jobs that are open today? High level job postings don't attract the "junk"[6] candidates that lower level infrastructure jobs will. So odds are good that you'll have at least 20+ strong competitors for each job at your level.

The point here is that you will need to put some thought into how employers will be searching for you, so that you can be found in the crowd. You need to position yourself *virtually* so that the internet will "index" you correctly and so that your name comes up in the relevant searches for candidates like you.

So, yes, even for high level executives, it's now about the internet and the race to notoriety.

Found versus hired

The other night at a dinner party, I was discussing the book with a powerful woman who had been a very successful campaign manager, an executive director, and a change agent inside city government.

Her comment to me was:

"Yes, I know the internet is the way that recruiting is going, but if I were looking for a job, I would want to be interviewed and hired by a person instead of by a computer, thank you very much."

It struck me then that I need to back up a bit and define this "internet indexing" phraseology.

---

[6] A "junk" candidate is not a bad person. It is a reference to a resume submitted for unemployment reporting purposes and has little or no relevant experience for the job.

Google, LinkedIn, Facebook, and Twitter are not the forums where you will get *hired*. They are the channels through which you will be *found and screened* before any decision is made to bring you in for an in-person interview.

For example, when you were an employed executive, you probably hired a recruiter at some point to perform a search for an opening you had in your department. Chances are the recruiter told you it would take 90 days to perform such a search. The 90 days were consumed by hundreds of phone calls to sources and contacts to get referrals to prospective candidates.

These were followed by dozens of phone conversations with those referrals, and then some skills testing or personality fit testing.

In the second month, the headhunter might have met face-to-face with a dozen of those candidates for "corporate culture" fit assessment. And he might have talked to references about the person's business behavior.

Now, through online search tools such as Google, Bing, and Yahoo, and social media sites such as LinkedIn, coupled with online due diligence tools (discussed ahead), this traditional process can be reduced from 90 days to about 4 weeks.

As a candidate, this is important to you, because you can now get in front of the human decision-makers faster if you and all your asset value can be found more quickly.

So these tools are not *replacing* the human decision factor. They are simply the new shortcuts for *finding you* in the first place so that you can be considered for the job.

Even the big five retained search firms use these online search tools to find you and to do their due diligence about you as one of the steps in their process.

Headhunters were the first ones to discover how to use these tools for recruiting, but employers have now figured out how easy and cost-effective it is to use these tools themselves for most of their job openings.

We'll discuss exactly how they do this in Chapter 4.

Due diligence

OK. On to the scary part. Due diligence.

Not only will the employer or recruiter use the internet to find you more quickly, but they also will know these things about you before they meet you:

- Chronological work history
- Address, phone number, and former addresses
- Hobbies and interests
- Writing skills
- Physical appearance
- Community involvement
- Political contributions
- Friends and family data
- Business network population and content

For example, I can go to any of the "people search" tools like Intelius, or Dogpile, or People Lookup and type in a name and city.

For *free* I can see where Henry Q. Wilson has lived before, how old he is, and who his relatives are. See Figure 1-2.

For a whopping $1.95, I can also get his address, phone number and date of birth.

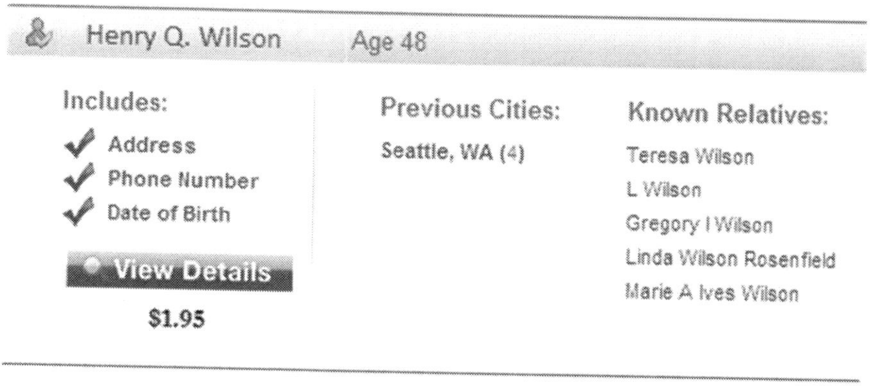

Henry Q. Wilson	Age 48	
Includes:	**Previous Cities:**	**Known Relatives:**
✔ Address	Seattle, WA (4)	Teresa Wilson
✔ Phone Number		L Wilson
✔ Date of Birth		Gregory I Wilson
View Details		Linda Wilson Rosenfield
$1.95		Marie A Ives Wilson

Figure 1-2

Here are some sites that will scare the pants off you:

ISearch: Type in a person's name and State and this site captures data from the web and displays it for anyone to see... for free. This data can include their home address, phone number, age, spouse name, criminal history, and even a map to their home. See Figure 1-3:

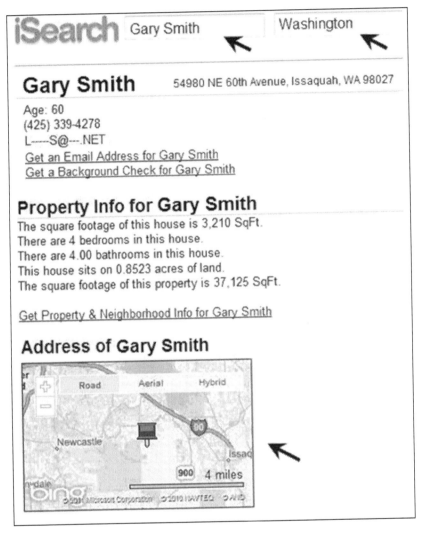

Figure 1-3

The problem with some of these sites is that the information is not necessarily true!

If you go to that same site, www.isearch.com and type in William H. Gates + Washington, you'll get a bunch of fake data about him *as if* it were true.

There are sites that exist for the sole purpose of helping anyone find dirt on another person or company like www.DirtSearch.org.

Other sites that may turn up "digital dirt" on you, intentionally or not, are Flickr, Spokeo, PeopleLookup, MyLife, LiveJournal (which has 35 million online journals and communities), GovPeopleSearch.net, and lookupanyone.com.

A great deal of this book is dedicated to how you can control what people see about you when they do find you.

Right now you may be thinking this is all scare tactics and psychobabble... or that we are suggesting a lot of unnecessary detail, *or* that this is relevant only for lower level infrastructure job seekers.

Not so.

Let me assure you that everything in this book (and in our Executive Program) is meant to help you create and control your online brand and short-cut the screening process... not elongate it.

This is the new reality. You're going to have to deal with it, or be left behind.

As proof, a recent Wall Street Journal article[7] discusses the growing use of social networks for candidate searching by employers.

"SAIC has asked its 125 U.S. recruiters to find candidates for analyst, engineering, and other jobs on professional social networks instead [of job boards]."

And the Corporate Executive Board, a business consulting firm, says that 24% of the companies they survey say they will do the same.

The same article discusses a large financial services company's recruiting woes.

---

[7] Wall Street Journal Jan. 19, 2011 "Recruiters Rethink Online Playbook"

The journalist reports that this employer is "currently reorganizing its recruiting staff to better handle the **tens of thousands of applications** it receives in a given month. Instead of using senior recruiters to filter through the company's applicants, **lower-level screeners process them first** and only hand off the most-qualified. A separate set of recruiters **actively searches for more experienced candidates** who aren't likely to come in through a job board."

This article is a pointed reference to what is happening in the search market today:

1. Companies are swamped with applicants at all levels.
2. The bulk of the screening is being done by low-level recruiters (who are simply looking for keyword match to their job description).
3. The recruiters who are tasked with finding senior level candidates are *not* looking on Monster and CareerBuilder. *But* they are using LinkedIn and other online networks to find you.

LinkedIn

Since we refer to LinkedIn several times in this book for its importance in your job search, we will describe it here briefly and go into considerable depth later as it relates to each chapter.

LinkedIn is just one (and the largest with over 100 million members) of the "professional social networks" on the market. As of January 2011, LinkedIn includes members from all 2010 Fortune 500 companies, and its hiring solutions were used by 69 of the Fortune 100 companies as of December 31, 2010[8].

Here's how LinkedIn works:

You invite your direct business contacts to join your LinkedIn community online. They are your 1st degree of connections. When they accept your invitation, you can then view their online profiles.

---

[8] From http://press.linkedin.com/about/

In addition, you can see all of *their* 1st degree contacts, who become *your* 2nd degree contacts. And so on. See Figure 1-4.

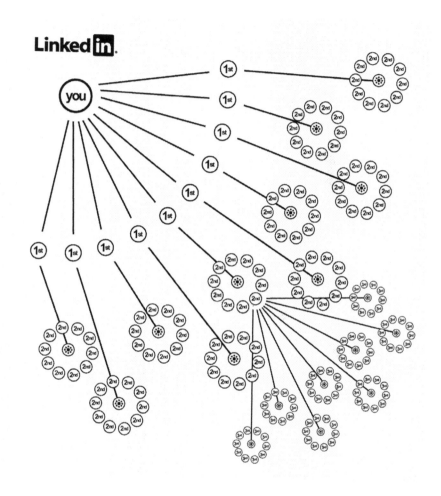

Figure 1-4

In fact, LinkedIn is so huge that it returns an overwhelming amount of information when you search there (for companies, for jobs, for discussion groups to join, and for people to connect with), because of its sheer size. This is a good thing for global reach, but can be overwhelming in broad subject area searches, like "company=Cisco," for instance.

So, for researchers and job seekers who are looking for a smaller universe of targeted subject matter, there are a growing number of smaller "niche" online membership sites cropping up. These allow business people with a common niche specialty or industry focus to join and virtually connect to share information and ask questions in that particular realm of interest.

For instance, Sermo.com is a medical network where doctors share info and opinions. Reuters even has a social network site for fund managers, traders and analysts.

It's important to know about social networks and to do some research on the networks in your industry, since those are the online sites where employers and recruiters will look for you.

We'll talk more about this in Chapters 4, 5 and 9.

CHAPTER 2

DEFINE

Can you define your unique business strengths?

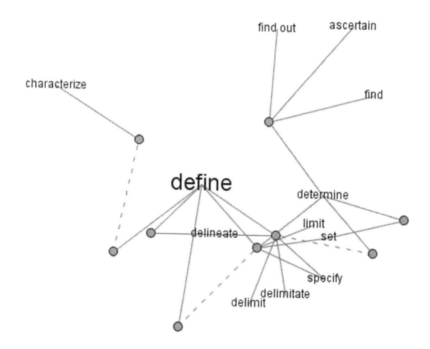

Before we launch you into the world of online search and social networks, we need to make sure you have a very competitive resume and profile.

Things to keep in mind:

- Recruiters do not make any money spending time with you to write your resume, unless they are outplacement specialists (those who are hired by companies who have just laid off executives to help them through the transition of the exit.)

- Recruiters do not help you figure out what you're good at.

- It is not an interviewer's job to figure out what you might be good at. It is your job. Don't expect anyone to read between the lines of your "synopsis" resume and surmise what you can do. The days of tantalizing hiring authorities with mysteriously clever cover letters are gone. The days of bringing you in for an informational interview to swap stories are gone. You'll never get an interview if your documentation pieces (including resumes and online profiles) aren't strong and packed with data and specific accomplishments.

- Your buddies, your wife, your neighbors don't really know what you're good at unless they've worked directly with or for you. Don't expect them to network you to a job unless you give them a very specific view of your skills, your accomplishments and your current objective – in a format they can easily distribute.

I can't tell you how many emails I've received over the last 20 years from "Louis" that say *"Hey, Colleen, can you meet with my neighbor/buddy/brother-in-law? He is looking for a job."* My response is, *"What does he do?"* The inevitable response is *"I don't really know, but I think he is in some type of Marketing."* This becomes a low priority for me as a recruiter, since I am not working any searches right now that need marketing expertise.

Remember, recruiters don't find jobs for people. However, if Louis were to send me a killer resume of a real player, it might be to my advantage as a recruiter to introduce this referral to a current client of mine who seems to be a good personality/energy/philosophy/expertise match for them. In that case, it makes me, as a recruiter, look like I'm connected to really top-notch definitive problem solvers.

Narrow and Deep

Before you can write an effective resume, or develop a comprehensive online presence, you must understand the unique set of knowledge and skills that you bring to the table.

In the Executive Program, we have evolved an in-depth exercise we call "Narrow and Deep." We walk an executive candidate through the process to *narrow* skill areas down to specific problems he is good at solving because of *deep* knowledge of the subject. We can walk *you* through this process. But it's outlined here in case you feel you can get started on your own. Here are the steps:

- Take an Assessment Test
- Talk with an assessment expert for the total picture of your scores
- Map out your strengths chronologically
- List the problems you've solved more than once
- Discover the silver thread in your career
- Position the reason for your exit from your last employer

Assessments

Find a high end professional assessment test that has serious validity testing behind it, and is focused on job-relatedness (i.e. not just a personality test). We use a few different assessments. One is a series called PreVue (www.prevueassessments.com), and another is Profiles (www.profilesinternational.com) but you can use any highly validated (proven on thousands of people) testing tool.

The results from these tests provide another set of data in determining your Narrow and Deep specialty areas – information about your abilities, your motivations, and your personality. (See Figure 2-1).

These types of test results also serve as an analytical tool to add credence to what you say in an interview.

For instance, if a hiring manager is listening to you talk about your prowess as a Director of Client Services, he can easily believe it from your "10" skill score on "Working with People" combined with your high score on "Working with Words" and being "Conscientious."

The scoring looks something like Figure 2-1:

Abilities	1	2	3	4	5	6	7	8	9	10	
General Abilities						(6)					High
Working With Numbers						(6)					High
Working With Words					(5)						High
Working With Shapes							(7)				High

Motivation/Interests	1	2	3	4	5	6	7	8	9	10	
Working with People						(6)					High
Working with Data						(6)					High
Working with Things								(8)			High

Personality	1	2	3	4	5	6	7	8	9	10	
Diplomatic						(6)					Independent
Cooperative						(6)					Competitive
Submissive						(6)					Assertive
Spontaneous							(7)				Conscientious
Innovative							(7)				Conventional
Reactive							(7)				Organized
Introvert					(5)						Extrovert
Self-Sufficient			(3)								Group-Oriented
Reserved							(7)				Outgoing
Emotional						(6)					Stable
Restless						(6)					Poised
Excitable						(6)					Relaxed
Frank						(6)					Social Desirability

Figure 2-1

After you have taken an online assessment, arrange to talk with an assessment expert about the findings. He will be able to translate your scores in a way that will be useful to you in validating some perceived strengths, or in discussing certain combinations of scores that point to recurring problem areas or overlooked areas of talent.

Many of these tests can also provide a report that overlays your scores onto a list of job functions for which you are a high percentage match. These are particularly helpful for executives who may have forgotten a job function they were particularly good at, or that provided extreme job satisfaction in the past.

Map out your strengths

Sit down with your resume or list of chronological jobs you've had and determine the one or two things that you were consistently good at. Which problems were you always called upon to solve, since you did it well? What issues were always the same at your last 3 jobs, becoming easier to solve each time you faced them?

For instance, are you always the elephant hunter who closes the big partner deals through your industry connections? Are you the one who consistently just knows how to right-size a struggling company? Or maybe you always bring the funding with you, or bring the killer team with you? Maybe you're the peace maker – the executive that everyone trusts to remain neutral and level-headed.

When you come to me and say *"Oh, I'm a generalist"* or *"I'm open"* or *"I don't want to limit myself"* I am translating that to:

I'm desperate
I'm still wondering what I want to be when I grow up
Once I get into a company, they'll figure out where I fit
I'm going through mid-life crisis
I'm not a planner
I'm simply an opportunist

Or finally, *I'm really not good at anything. I just wing it.*

The candidate usually thinks he is coming across as:

Being a Gordon Gekko type risk-taker
Being multi-talented
Being mysterious and exciting
Being easy to work with
Being broadly marketable

So who are you really and what is the objective of your quest? What is the size of company or division that best suits you? Are you more of an idea person or an implementer? Do you like to lead projects or follow a good lead? Do you want lots of customer contact or not? Do you do well in high-stress, fast-paced environments or are you looking to slow down and add balance to your life?

Problems you've solved

At this stage in your career, you've undoubtedly solved many problems. But telling me or a hiring manager that your strength is "taking corporate problems and breaking them down into solvable parts" is not specific enough.

I don't know how many executives I've met with who have said:

"I don't do resumes. Just get me in front of the CEO and we can talk peer-to-peer about his problems and go from there..."

So how are you planning to get in front of the CEO? Recruiters will only put you in touch with their clients if you're a match to a specific opening. Consulting firms will put you in front of a CEO if you have a specific history of solving a specific problem they are contracted to solve.

So you need to get Narrow and Deep about which problems you solve better than anyone else.

What employers care about

Today, employers want to know <u>four</u> things about you, no matter what your job function: General Manager, CEO, VP Sales, COO, CFO, or head of your own consulting firm:

1. How have you INCREASED REVENUES/PROFITABILITY?
2. How have you DECREASED COSTS?
3. What PROBLEMS have you SOLVED and HOW?
4. How CREATIVE are you?

You will see these again in Chapter 3 in discussions about writing resumes in a way that brings your total asset value into one document.

But keep these four questions in mind when you go through the exercise of determining your specific strengths.

If you think you have a particular talent, go back to this list and see if that strength directly affects a company's bottom line in one of these four areas.

Useful exercises

As a help, I have included a list of questions that will help you get rolling in your own "greatness."

Did you ever:

- get promoted in any of your jobs?
- hire a superstar?
- reduce the cost of sales in any way?
- change or update an existing manufacturing process for the better?
- present a plan of your own that was then adopted?
- negotiate a more profitable arrangement with a vendor?
- create or change your company's mission statement?
- submit a game-changing report to the Board?
- bring in new technology that increased productivity?
- acquire or merge a company which led to increased profits or just continued survival?
- rebuild a failing department?
- launch a new product on time and under budget?
- uncover a major accounting error to the company's benefit?

Also, sit down with your co-worker, your old boss, your protégé, your biggest critic, your best friend, and ask them (I know this sounds hokey but it works) "What makes me so special? What am I good at?"

Chances are, at one time or another, you've bragged (okay, just stated the facts!) to one of these people about a problem you solved or a particularly brilliant idea you put into play at the office. They will remember. Work from these.

Here's another simple exercise. Take a generic org chart like the one on the next page in Figure 2-2 and, starting from the top, list one issue you've discussed with an executive in each of these departments. Then try to remember the role you may have played in solving these issues, specifically.

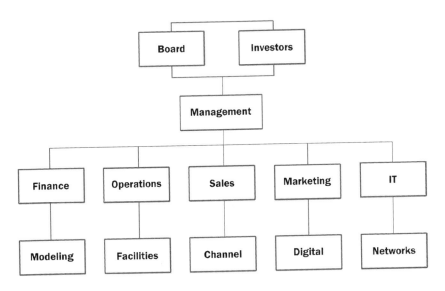

Figure 2-2

For instance, as the VP of Strategy for a global company, you may have spoken with the CFO about a new expansion solution, or suggested contract wording in the company's favor.

Or as the Head of Human Resources, you may have implemented a succession planning strategy that helped to retain critical executives.

If you've done similar strategic feats more than once, these may be specialties that you take for granted, but that can really affect the bottom line of your next employer.

Here's another process we step you through in our Executive Program (See Figure 2-3).

It is a complex exercise that cannot be sufficiently explained in a chapter since it's usually an all-day session, but is included here to help you expand your thinking about your proven strengths by looking at your experiences in a more structured way.

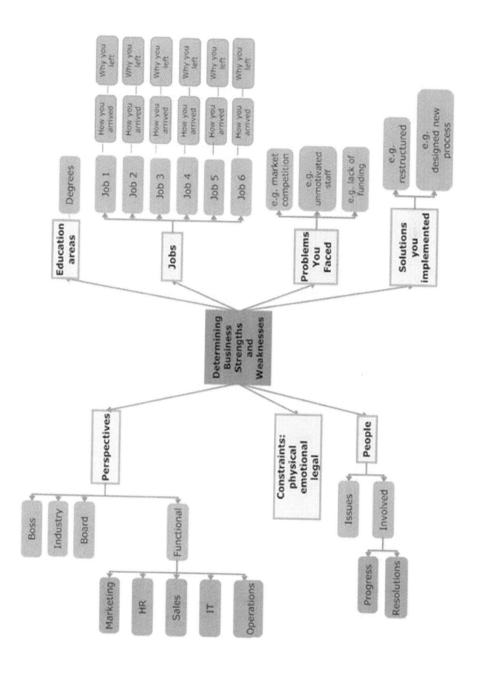

Figure 2-3

Start with any advanced degrees you may hold. How about patents?

Next, for each job:

- How did you get there? If you were constantly recruited into your jobs by former bosses, then that is huge asset value and should be highlighted.

- What were the problems facing you in that job? How did you resolve them?

- For each company you worked for, what were the business perspectives and goals of the Board and Management? Did they match your own? Did you bring a different and more productive perspective that resulted in positive action?

- What personal and business constraints did you have in each job? What were the hurdles and how did you overcome them?

This can be a time-consuming exercise, but well worth it when the interview cycle occurs. You will already have your answers and "proof stories" for those conversations.

CHAPTER 3

AGGREGATE

How do you translate all your asset value into a resume today?

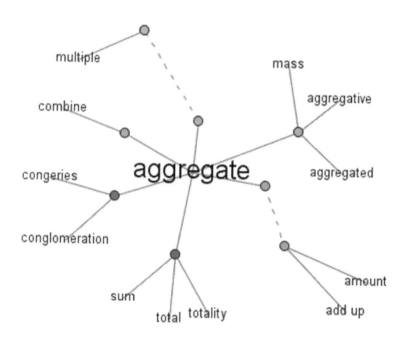

Now that you've done your Narrow and Deep exercises and have determined what you are truly good at, and have examples to prove it, you can start to aggregate all this data into one document: your resume. This document also forms the basis of your online profile which we discuss in Chapter 4.

No longer is a resume just a list of past jobs and education. It is a book cover that says *"Open and read on!" "Follow this incredible story line!" "See how I can solve that pesky problem you've been losing sleep over!"*

Every job opening today receives more than 100 resumes. Chapter 4 talks about how to position yourself in this crowd. But first you need a document to place out there in your positioning strategy.

And yes, "networking" (See Chapter 10) is the new watchword in job search, but, again, you first have to start with a validation document (today's resume) that serves a few different purposes:

1. Shows your progression through your career
2. Reflects your personality and drive
3. Provides anecdotes as examples of your accomplishments
4. Provides numbers and timelines that speak to your ability to solve problems quickly and with great ROI
5. Tells the reader *how* you obtained each job and *why* you left
6. Can include pertinent accolades from 3rd parties who witnessed your talent
7. Tells *clearly* how you approach and solve problems
8. Provides a fully-loaded document you can give to those with whom you will network, including friends and family who really have no idea what you really do at work

How many pages are appropriate for a resume?

The one-page synopsis is a thing of the past. And now that I've said this, please put your teeth back in, take a valium and read on.

First of all, length is really irrelevant compared to content. Put yourself in the shoes of a hiring manager for a moment and I'll explain why. The hiring authority must sift through dozens, or even hundreds of paper or online resumes to choose a first list of candidates who *might* be qualified.

Give him what he needs to count you "in." And not by giving *fewer words*, but more meat. When you synopsize or just give hints of your history and talents (thinking you'll get to elaborate in person), you run these risks:

1)   You *assume* the reader will read between the lines and come up with the correct evaluation of what it is you can do, or will do. As a recruiter, I get very frustrated with this. I can't tell whether you are lazy, modest, or have no idea why anyone would want to hire you.

2)   You *assume* the reader knows the size and structure, the product or service and the marketplace of your current and past employers.

3)   You *assume* the reader will be impressed by your title(s) and know where you fit in the hierarchy of responsibility in your corporate structure.

4)   You *assume* that using vague business platitudes will "sort of cover every possible job opening" and therefore not limit your chances.

5)   You *assume* the reader is in the business of using his own time and imagination to try to figure out what your potential could be within his company; in other words, what his company could do for *you* to help *your* growth.

When you make these assumptions, you are putting the responsibility (the "work") on the hiring manager. Your chances of being chosen for an interview are 50 – 50 at best, because the reader can only relate to your verbiage from his own experience in the business world. Hiring managers are human. They have their own pre-conceived ideas about certain companies, titles and resumes, *and* their own time table pressures for filling positions. Don't limit your chances by vagueness.

Take Control. Be Specific. Don't make more work for hiring managers than they already have. Believe me – this won't limit you. The only "limiting" this will do is to limit the waste of everyone's time.

Unless you have only 1 or 2 short jobs to relate, a resume can easily be 2 pages without being overkill. The longest resume I have seen without any fluff is 8 pages. Of course, this included 3 addendum pages of appropriate publications, languages, and key business relationships, and was a paper customized for a Marketing position that called for detailed technical writing skills.

The point here is that if you write a very full, factual, chronological resume you should be covered. A skimmer-type of hiring manager should be able to skim and see the important facts jump out.

35

A detail person will be able to glean the answers to all his basic questions and also get a good sense of you as a person.

The objective statement

Forget the Objective Statement – unless you do it right. Now, this doesn't mean to forget your objective. You need to have an objective. But we will discuss that later in the "Silver Thread" section of this chapter.

Look at this objective statement:

"To obtain a high-level position in a stable, forward-thinking, growth-oriented, well-funded company where my true potential can be fully realized, and my experience and skills can be utilized to attain the long-term goals of your company."

Blech! This is what all Objective Statements tend to read like. This is fluff. Don't insult the interviewer.

First of all, those companies are rather scarce these days. Secondly, WHAT ARE YOU, NUTS?!! Do you think everyone *else* uses:

"To obtain a low-level position in an unstable, backward-thinking, static, financially shaky company where my potential will probably not be realized and my background will have no relevance."

Let's face it, employers are looking for someone who fits *their* objective, and it is *your* responsibility to do the research of the potential employer's goals and objectives, and it is your responsibility to accept or reject an offer from a company that may or may not have the same values and goals as yours.

Remember to think of your job search as a win-win endeavor. You are not begging for a job and the employer is not desperate to have you. You have specific strengths, financial goals and intangible needs that must be addressed in your next position. Excuse my preaching, but you are truly a unique set of energy, opinions, dislikes, skills, preferences and idiosyncrasies.

You are the only one who can take care to see that all your needs are met. And, you are the only one who can justify yourself to a potential employer, no matter how many glowing references you have and how silver-tongued a headhunter may be representing you.

So, if you insist on using an objective statement, model it like these which are about *them* and not you.

"My objective is to be the #1 support person for the CEO of [your company], as I have in the past -- defining and implementing solid reporting, modeling, analysis, and general accounting strategies and their procedures which will consistently upgrade and maintain the financial health of [your company]."

"To become your most creative problem solver in the Marketing Department using my proven ability to effectively communicate the right messages, present nascent solution options, negotiate on behalf of the company, and assist in closing profitable business deals with impeccable business ethics and win-win results."

What about a summary statement?

There is nothing wrong with a *Good* summary statement at the beginning of a resume. But how often do you see a "summary" like this:

- *Excellent communicator*
- *Proven Leader*
- *Goal oriented*
- *Revenue Producer*
- *Problem Solver*
- *Attention to Detail*
- *Ability to Motivate and Drive Teams*
- *Ability to Bring Order to Chaos*

or this:

"A seasoned professional with 20 years experience in Sales and Marketing in high tech industries."

First, they are boring, unimaginative and over-used. Out of the 20 or 30 resumes I receive every day, I must see these at least a dozen times.

Second, a summary must be exactly that - a summary. In other words, the reader should expect to see specific validations of these statements later in the text of the resume.

If you present yourself in the Summary as an excellent communicator and your resume does not *later* say...

"Chosen out of 6 others to present new product lines to Board Room audiences and the media"

...then chances are I won't have any way of knowing whether your mother thinks you communicate well or a professional resume writer gave you a form on which you checked off nice-sounding skills.

The second statement above about being a "seasoned professional" says nothing to me other than that the candidate has been around awhile. It would help to put in a word like "successful" before "experience" but it would still be trite. Besides, in a Sales resume, the reader usually jumps immediately to the text as the success barometer. Therefore, an appropriate summary section on a sales resume might be 4 bullets of performance awards, and consistent quota percentages.

The four basic questions

We mentioned this in the last chapter. Employers are only interested in these four things:

1) How have you INCREASED REVENUES/PROFITABILITY?
2) How have you DECREASED COSTS?
3) What PROBLEMS have you SOLVED and HOW?
4) How CREATIVE are you?

The first two questions are centuries old, but extremely relevant in today's economy. And the 3rd and 4th points above could not be more critical, as many more companies today are facing recent or impending layoffs, bankruptcies, reorganizations, new legislation and tax issues, stiffer global competition and smaller windows of opportunity within which to market a niche product.

Your resume needs to reflect your savvy in these arenas. Employers no longer have the luxury to hire someone with a toothy smile and firm handshake to "train on the job." You must bring problem-solving skills and creativity to a job. And, you must reflect those skills on your resume.

Be sure to address each and every one of these questions in your resume.

For a salesman, it is fairly simple to answer #1 by simply stating quota achievements. For a CEO hired to turn around a company's performance, it is obvious that #1 and #2 will be addressed in his resume (but you would be surprised at the number of high level executives who don't quantify on their resume). For example, these bullets attribute no kudos at all to the author:

"Oversaw sales and support for information management systems in the Northwest"

"Consolidated sales activities into one organization"

SO WHAT?

What *resulted* from these tasks that you performed? What benefit did your actions provide for your employer in bottom line dollars? The writer is assuming that the reader will do the work of translating these features into the correct benefit statement. On the flip side, the following leaves nothing to figure out:

"Reduced expenses by $680,000 through the consolidation of separate facilities and the elimination of 7 functions in a restructuring of the organization."

For a Product Manager, it is slightly harder to relate day-to-day activities to bottom line but here are some excellent examples:

"Rolled out one product a month early by employing concurrent engineering." (Problem solving and creativity)

"Raised seed capital to jump start sales effort in consumer channels by finding an investor and building a relationship." (Creativity and increasing revenue)

"Implemented a demo program which was widely acknowledged by the field sales reps as making the difference between winning and losing sales. Sales volume increase was $1MM in the first year of its use." (Problem solving/creativity/increasing revenue)

"Raised gross margins from 35% to 55% on new product version by reducing costs of goods and assembly. Industry average for gross margins is 42.5% for companies of similar size." (Cost reducing/Profit increasing)

Notice the use of the operative word "by." She, the candidate, clearly understands cause and effect and is tuned into Bottom Line. She also is sensitive to the fact that the reader may not have a frame of reference for gross margins in her particular industry.

On the other hand, in a Marketing position, you often are floating in a sea of intangibles and it's difficult to come up with direct cause-and-effect relationships between your work and "dollars in." Look at these good examples:

"Eliminated channel conflict by pioneering a lead- and revenue-sharing scheme for all channels of distribution."

"Revitalized company name by refocusing corporate image on innovative technology."

"Redesigned trade show booth to match all corporate literature, presenting a consistent message and delivering the statement that my company is certainly alive and well."

"Created a vehicle to collect end-user information in order to cross-sell product lines and overcame the problem of limited access to customers when selling through distributors. End-user registrations poured in and a database of hundreds of customers grew in 4 months' time."

A Business Development Manager has no quotas per se but must be able to relate his activities directly to the Bottom Line:

"Secured development contracts and OEM relationships worth $5MM over 3 years by pursuing independent software developer projects with Microsoft, Intel, IBM."

"Led the project to port the product over to WIN95 platform in order to take advantage of the magnitude of difference in the installed base of 800,000 3.1 to 18 million WIN95 users. Placed the products in the mainstream, which boosted sales 130% in the first year."

Now question #3 on Problem Solving, and question #4 on Creativity, are significant ones in today's economy. Employers are not necessarily looking for people who have been "good boys and girls" and stayed with one large company for 15 years.

More often, companies today who are looking for employees are the objects of an extremely fast-paced development or manufacturing cycle, extremely hot competitive environment, the pressure of a short roll-out-to-pay-back timeframe, high risk factors, low budgets, and flighty investors. These companies need employees who have a track record of success, yes, but "success under duress" is a more commonly sought after quality.

Good examples would include a CFO who has been through a merger; a salesman who has successfully switched from direct to channel sales or vice versa; a product manager who has saved the day by garnering a partnership for a customized (lucrative) application; a salesman who has sought out and captured a new vertical market for his product; a plant manager who has championed the latest automation technology; a manager who has solved a sticky personnel issue.

Get the picture?

Now, the next section will help to start putting this all together.

Format

First of all, I urge you not to go to a "resume house" or "resume writer." This defeats the whole purpose of a resume as a "unique view of a candidate" and "the first impression of a candidate's own ability to sell or market himself."

Remember, you Sales and Marketing types, employers are not dumb. They are thinking "if you can't sell yourself, you can't sell my product and if you can't market yourself, you can't market my company."

Admittedly, writing your own resume is *not* fun and *not* easy.

However, I urge you to grow your own resume. It is a lot of hard work up front, but it will be with you the rest of your days as your unique flag to wave whenever needed. It will be the best and truest description of YOU that has ever been written (yes, you can will it to your children or to science). It is an exercise on paper but more importantly, a mental positioning of your self-confidence. When you have it completed, you will know.

You will feel in your gut that it truly represents your best self. And, lastly, the work up front saves a lot of sweat-time in the interview (which you undoubtedly will obtain from such a well written resume!). It will help both you and the interviewer over that awful first 20 minutes of:

"What exactly did that company do? What was your reporting structure? Who was your market? Why did you leave? How did you get that job? How many people did you manage? What was your quota?" etc., etc.

This is the first 20 minutes in which the interviewer is trying to find a reason *not* to hire you, *not* to believe your resume, and get on to the next interview.

It is also the time when the candidate cannot get comfortable in the chair, hasn't figured out the agenda of the interviewer, wonders when he'll get his chance to make his pitch (which, by the way, may never come) and wishes he hadn't wasted his time coming to this interview at all, because obviously the interviewer can't see how special he is from the beginning so forget *her* and *this job*!!

For a resume, the "start from the beginning and tell me all about yourself" approach is out. LIFO (Last-In-First-Out) is in. After your summary or "overview" statement, if you felt you needed one, start your resume out right away with job history, beginning with current position first and going back in time from here. The most relevant experience you will have to the job you want is your most current. Or that's the way we generally think as employers and recruiters.

List each job in the same format, with the same typeface, indentations, etc.

Be sure to state the full company name, the division you worked for, the exact dates of employment, and your specific title. Also add in parentheses the name of the parent or holding company or the name of the largest stockholder, if known.

A word about dates. In general, the people in this country read left to right. Place your dates of employment in the left margin next to company name – for skimmers to skim. If you had more than one position in the same company, place "position dates" after the position title (on the same line to the right as in the example below) or in some indented fashion so it is clearly a subset of your tenure at the one company. You don't want to run the risk of a "skimmer" discarding your resume because of to perceived job-hopping.

(1992 – 2006)
SOLITRON DEVICES, INC., West Palm Beach, FL
($10M Defense contractor that manufactures discrete electronic components)
- Production Operations Manager **(1996 - 2006)**
- Product Line Manager **(1992 – 1996)**

Regarding company name, always enter a one or two line description of the company. Even if you think it is an insult to the intelligence of the reader, do it. In this day and age, the hi-tech industry has too many small spin-offs, start ups, and unrelated divisions to make the assumption that the reader will know exactly what you were involved in.

Even if it is IBM, put in a few lines of description about the company as it relates to the job you are interviewing for. For example:

> IBM   (1997 – 2003)
> **(The division which markets mid-range manufacturing systems in the price range of $10K - $100K to Fortune 1000 companies.)**

Don't leave things out, thinking they will be good conversation pieces for the interview. Sure enough, the interviewer will either skip over it, leaving you no place to make your pitch, or will make a statement or an assumption about your job history that is incorrect. This only puts both of you in a no-win situation since the interviewer may be embarrassed or annoyed, and this is no time for you to "one-up" the interviewer by your hidden knowledge.

Employers are looking for the common ground that you both share, not your potential to do a job you've never done.

A word about titles. Many companies have their own unique internal hierarchies with attendant titles. A hiring manager at one company may not know what a "Level 3" position means at another company. Likewise, a Sales Engineer could be more of a technical position at one company and a heavily commissioned sales position at another.

A CFO title could simply mean the company bookkeeper (I once had a CFO who called himself the OFO - "only financial officer") or, on the other hand, the VP Finance title could actually have COO and CIO responsibilities as well.

So never assume that a hiring manager knows where your title puts you. Either make it very clear in your ensuing "Responsibilities and Accomplishments" section or put a short layman's description following the title. This will save everyone a lot of time and possible miscommunication.

And never make yourself out to be something you are/were not. The global village is now too small for you ever to get away with it. On the other hand, you may want to play down some facts. A high level candidate I was speaking to couldn't seem to get an interview.

Looking at his resume, I noticed he listed himself as a "Corporate Officer" on nearly every position in the last 10 years. This was scaring people off for two reasons. Employers perceive him as too far along the food chain to have many productive years left. In addition, he was limiting himself on paper. Employers perceive he will only be interested in a Corporate Officer position in the future.

Similarly, a long-time friend came to me last week who has owned his own construction company for the last 25 years. His partner wants to retire, but my friend can't afford to buy him out in this economy so he thinks he should shutter his business and put his resume out there. The first problem is that his resume lists his title as OWNER for 25 years.

Let's go through what the hiring manager on the other side of the desk is thinking about this resume:

"This guy wants my job."
"This guy can't be managed since he's done whatever he wants for 25 years."
"As soon as the economy picks up, this guy is outa here."

We have changed my friend's title now to "VP Field Operations and Job Superintendent" and he is being seen as a non-threatening peer on many LinkedIn Groups and social communities where he is building his brand.

Accomplishments versus Responsibilities

Always separate job description or "responsibilities" from your particular accomplishments in a job.

For example, these are Responsibilities (always list in order of importance):

- *Responsible for $1.2MM quota*
- *Manage 15 sales reps*
- *Manage product through roll-out*
- *Analyze new investment opportunities*
- *Support national distribution network*
- *Coordinate promotional activities*
- *Speak at industry conferences*
- *Draft mechanical connection details*
- *Detail electrical schematics*
- *Responsible for order entry and billing*
- *Install telecommunications equipment*
- *Design LAN/WAN/PC environment*
- *Develop training standards*

They are simply descriptions of the job title duties...responsibilities that anyone with the title should take on. On the other hand, accomplishments are those things that you, as a unique contributor, have done with the job title in answer to The Four Basic Questions laid out on page 38 (increase revenues, decrease costs, solve problems, show creativity).

These are Accomplishments (again, be sure to list in order of greatest importance):

- *Developed and implemented the marketing plan, generating an unprecedented $14MM of new business within an 18 month time frame.*
- *Obtained financing for a new and unique $3MM piece of medical equipment, providing a return on investment of over 20%.*
- *Youngest salesman in the 20 year history of the company to be promoted to Regional Manager.*
- *Managed and designed a WAN/LAN/PC environment (from 0 PCs to 230+ PCs and 6 LANs over 5 years).*
- *Successfully downsized a corporation's accounting and tax processing from a large minicomputer environment to "the Cloud" - on time and under budget.*
- *Obtained approval on 48 of 50 major transactions presented to Senior Investment Committee, after researching and analyzing over 300 investment opportunities.*
- *Improved customer service with 7 consecutive years of 99%+ order fill.*
- *Initiated and designed pricing structure increasing order volume and profits while decreasing distribution costs.*
- *Instituted a Customer Truckload Allowance Incentive Program resulting in distribution cost savings of $1MM in one year.*
- *Organized an elite corps of technical support personnel for customer liaison and incorporated highly technical equipment which resulted in 40% improvement in efficiency rate.*
- *Identified and penetrated new markets with existing products by initiating and implementing product packaging changes, generating over $3.5MM in sales the first year.*
- *Became the #1 producer within 6 months on a sales team of 10, and maintained that position for all 5 years.*
- *Simplified profiling process for Sales force by redesigning forms and having final documents completed in-house. This resulted in more sales calls and increased accuracy of waste samples.*
- *Completely overhauled my division in all areas of productization reducing order processing time from 13 hours to 1 hour, cutting error rate from 50% to under 2%, doubling orders processed – all with 20% less staff.*

Contrary to what we learned in college composition classes, it is highly appropriate to use actual numerical and monetary abbreviations instead of the spelled-out versions.

For example, "$14MM" and "33%" stand out in a resume much more (especially for those skimmers) than "fourteen million," or even $14 million, or 33 percent or thirty-three percent.

Accomplishments should be listed as bullets and obviously should be stated as clearly and strongly as possible. Beginning each accomplishment with an action word serves two purposes. One, action verbs cut right to the point. They are precise, strong, and set up a consistent, self-confident style for listing positive actions. Two, these verbs act as common bridge words in matching your experiences with those needed as background for future positions.

For instance, a start-up employer looking for a Marketing Manager of a very technical telecommunications product may be looking for experience words like:

- supervised
- managed
- designed
- implemented
- hired
- presented
- built the business plan for
- engineered
- wrote
- created
- led
- performed
- analyzed
- evaluated
- conducted
- prepared
- compiled
- installed
- established

Whereas, a hiring manager searching for an excellent sales rep would want to see:

- increased
- overcame
- sold
- uncovered
- won
- was awarded
- saved
- trained
- reduced
- achieved
- implemented
- conducted
- coordinated
- marketed
- set up
- top

A small company in financial trouble may be looking for key words in a potential CEO's resume such as:

- promoted
- overhauled
- reduced
- acquired
- dissolved
- cut
- doubled
- turned around
- guided
- led
- merged
- started
- reorganized

- expanded
- interfaced
- implemented
- recruited
- built
- taught
- arranged
- re-built
- planned
- hired
- developed
- programmed
- divested

These action words should be followed by the actual accomplishment description, its importance and how it was done. In other words, it is not sufficient to say:

"Analyzed market share of competition and identified shifts in the marketplace."

So what? WHAT RESULTS DID IT BRING ABOUT? At the same time, it is not enough just to say:

"Boosted sales by 132%" (How??)

Potential employers want to know 1) what you did that was so great, 2) how you did it (cause and effect) and 3) whether the methods and results could be directly transferable to their companies. They also want to know (and this is KEY) if *you know* what you did, know its impact, can effectively communicate it and recreate the same results for them.

If you can do this successfully on paper, your chances of obtaining an interview increase dramatically.

Employers like to see numbers. (And, again, don't spell them out. Use the real figures.) How big was your budget? What was your quota? What were your performance numbers? How many levels down were you from the top? How many people did you manage? How much time between your promotions? What were the revenues of your company/division?

For example:

"In addition to managing 5 direct reports, personally sold $5.4MM in new software (averaging $500K per system) in 21 months."

"Achieved 123% of 2009 new software sales quota of $20MM and exceeded total 2009 targeted revenue of $30MM for the Financial Software Division by approximately $7MM."

A word about TLAs (Three Letter Acronyms). Use acronyms in your resume "keyword" section, and in your LinkedIn "specialty" section, since recruiters will search for the acronyms as well as the spelled out version. We'll discuss this more in Chapter 4 where we teach you how recruiters and employers search for you online.

But when you are writing the textual "story" part of your resume, use them only when appropriate. *Know your audience !* Who will be reading your resume? When using TLAs, be sensitive to a hiring manager's scope. Don't use acronyms that are used only in a small niche market unless you explain them. It won't impress a hiring manager who is looking for a good communicator to get the impression that you are so narrowly focused.

For example, how clear is this description?

"Worked for XCS in the DRP and MRP solutions division."

It's rather like telling an inside joke.

On the other hand, you need to list all programming languages, protocols, manufacturing standards, and methodologies with which you are thoroughly familiar. *Do not* get caught up trying to list everything you've ever heard or read about. For instance if you've read a book on C# but never used it, don't put it in your specialty keyword section on your resume. This will backfire on you in an interview and even if you are wonderfully qualified in some other area, that hiring manager may not trust the balance of your resume. I've had candidates try to pass themselves off as international trade experts when all they have really done is run a small import service. This kind of sleight of hand wastes recruiters' time, and damages your credibility.

Again, employers don't hire on potential. They hire on *proof* that you can do/have done the job.

Keywords

Ok, let's talk about Keywords. The simplest explanation I give to people about the need for keywords is this:

Today, the first "screen" or "cut" is made by computers, not by people.

Every time you submit your resume for a job, it goes through the company's central screening system – usually called an Applicant Tracking System (ATS) or a Talent Acquisition System (TAS). These are recruiting software programs that "read" the textual content in a document and then take some action based on what they find.

To be equitable to all applicants, your resume is sent digitally through the employer's ATS along with the 99 other applicant resumes. If the program finds an abundance (we call it "density") of keywords in your resume that exactly match the keywords in the job description, then you make it onto the list to be considered.

The more exact the keyword match, and the more times those keywords are found in your document (again, "keyword density"), the higher you will appear on their potential match list.

Then, and only then, does a human look at your resume.

Rather frustrating to many, but until we breed humans who can read 100 resumes a day with complete comprehension, we need to use technology to help in screening.

All the more reason you need to learn the rules of the screening game, the first step of which is the keyword dance.

Now, remember this concept when we talk about SEO (search engine optimization) in Chapter 4.

SEO is the process of "optimizing" your resume for the ATS and "optimizing" your online profiles for the search engines. What this means *to you* is that you will be found by those who need you for the skills and experience that you possess.

Overcoming objections before they come up

There's no reason to feel you have to be perfect to get a job, or even to get an interview. But you do have to be believable. Don't make yourself out to be a water walker or you'll surely drown in the interview or the job itself.

Here are some red flags for my client companies and ways to overcome the inevitable objections before they ever come up:

The golden child

Nobody's perfect. Employers tend to do one of two things when they see a "perfect" person on paper. They will either bring the candidate in out of curiosity to poke holes in the perfection, or they will pass by out of fear that he is "too good to be true" (i.e., there must be some hidden horror.)

Failure is okay. In fact, many employers prefer a candidate who has hit the wall at 70 mph, picked himself up, dusted himself off and gone on with life having a new perception of speed. Bring up your failures, but be prepared to articulate what you have learned from them that you can bring to a new employer.

If you failed to make your quota in the year of your divorce, that's a valid failure. If you failed to motivate your sales reps to produce because you didn't believe in the product anymore, then say so. If your project was over budget and behind schedule, then explain the reasons in a positive 20/20 hindsight fashion.

Don't whine. Don't complain. And don't blame! (See the section later in this chapter on Anger). These are the kiss of death in an interview and on a resume. No matter what sort of bad luck has befallen you in the past, if you can present yourself as a better, stronger, clearer person because of it, you will be refreshing to an employer. One of the more clever ways I've seen a position "fraught with difficulties" described was this:

"As Product Marketing Manager, I met head-on the challenges of declining sales, an industry in disarray from the divestiture of AT&T and in economic recession (competitors at 60% of targeted income for first half of the year), a corporate identity so low profile that competitors and colleagues thought the company went under several years earlier, and an aging product line."

Remember that an employer's current situation probably involves at least a dozen of the problems you've already survived. Make yourself useful to him.

Job hopping

It used to be that you were a job hopper if you changed employers more than twice in your career. Nowadays, 4 years' tenure means stability. Times change. In today's hi-tech environment, it is considered industrious to spend 3 years each at several companies learning leading-edge secrets.

It makes you "marketable." Salesmen are lauded for jumping from base to higher base and from trend to trend. It makes them "marketable." A CEO that jumps from start-up to start-up as an IPO expert or a Business Development Specialist is in high demand. So don't apologize for short tenures but be able to put down on paper and verbalize your progression and your reasons.

A rather arrogant Sales candidate we'll call "Bob," handed me his one page job history that boldly listed 7 jobs in 12 years. It was no wonder he wasn't getting any bites on his resume. But after 20 minutes of pointed questions to him (the dreaded first 20 minutes!) I had a very cohesive "fast-riser" profile sketched out:

1. He hadn't really "job hopped." He had met the VP Marketing of AT&T at a luncheon, who was so impressed with him that he recruited him away from his first Sales job to penetrate 28 vertical market segments at AT&T. (Job change #1)

2. When a major client began a lawsuit against the company, Bob was nominated to go in and solve the client problems. (Job change #2)

3. He did such a great job solving the conflict in 6 months that he was given a promotion at AT&T. (Job change #3)

4. Soon after, the problem client recruited Bob to be their General Manager, since they had been so impressed with his problem-solving skills. (Job change #4)

5. The parent company of Bob's new employer began experiencing "financial difficulties" and dissolved his division. Bob was immediately picked up by a major financial software vendor (Job change #5), where he became the #1 rep.

51

6. A year later, this vendor company was acquired by its competitor, who did away with the line of software products Bob was selling. Bob was recruited into another software company where he is currently at 143% of quota in mid-year. (Job change #6)

This description is rather different from Bob's one-page list of short-tenured job titles. But even a cover letter from a recruiter will rarely be able to turn around the employer's first impression of this candidate as a job-hopper. Even if he eventually realizes Bob's true worth, he will wonder why Bob couldn't sell himself more effectively on his resume.

The simple use of the words "recruited by" and "recruited to" may overcome some of Bob's perceived sins. But this kind of job history may lend itself more to a functional resume than to a chronological one.

A functional resume is written as specific categories of qualifications or skills, rather than a historical view by job title. For instance, "Bob" could list his specific Responsibilities and Accomplishments under section headings of "Software Sales," "Management," and "Problem Solving." He has so many positive experiences and provable skills in these areas that the potential objection to short tenures can be overcome by this first-page impression.

The most common shortcoming of a functional resume is lack of specifics. Vagueness such as...

- *"Broad Range of Management Skills"*
- *"Comfortable Dealing at all Organizational Levels"*
- *"Introduced Innovative Sales Strategies"*
- *"Motivated coworkers to accomplish goals"*
- *"Monitored performance to ensure achievement"*

...simply uses up space, annoys the reader who is looking for results-oriented information, and won't get you an interview. *Be specific, , not coy.*

Reasons for leaving

This is one of the most stressful topics for an interview. So why not overcome it prior to the interview?

52

We just covered one method: the use of the words "Recruited to" and Recruited by." For example:

"Recruited as Vice President of Marketing to provide product and market vision and to transition a technology-driven, development company to a market-driven growth company."

"Recruited as Director of North American Sales to provide sales leadership and manage a team of 14 sales and support people in re-invigorating a stagnant sales situation."

Another simple yet often-overlooked word is "promoted." Use it where it is true. As we discussed before, a hiring manager may not be able to tell from a job title whether a move was a lateral one, a promotion, or even a demotion.

This job description leaves no questions in the reader's mind about the move:

"Promoted after 10 months to Managing Director of European subsidiary in London, England, to effect a major turnaround of a poorly performing operation and to consolidate a newly acquired company."

Now the sticky ones are:

- Quit
- Laid off
- Fired

First of all, I'd recommend *not* using these words on a resume. If you were fired, leave your explanations for the in-person interview. Don't bring it up on the resume.

BUT, I would suggest that you attach a list of references that includes past managers. (And, by the way, when alerting your references that they may be receiving calls, encourage them to not only stress your strengths, but to mention a few weaknesses also. Nobody's perfect, and it raises an employer's comfort level to get a REAL human profile.)

Then, in an interview, DO NOT BADMOUTH the company or person who fired you. Keep in mind that it is not unusual for human beings to be in conflict over matters of power, control, integrity and pay. So maybe you were caught in one of those situations.

The key is to let the wisdom gained from that experience shine through in the interview instead of the bitterness or blame.

Anger

A word about anger. It shows through your writing and your speech unless you are watchful about your communication. And no one wants to hire, let alone interview, an angry person -- *even if* your anger or bitterness is justified.

Check out the following paragraph that was used by a candidate as an explanation for his exit. He actually posted this in his online profile.

"The less said about this place, the better. The owner is crude, rude and disrespectful to his employees. Most employees fear for their jobs, or worse, brown nose. I only took a job here on the suggestion of an old friend, who ended up leaving herself a month after I came on board. They have no formal job descriptions, no formal review process, and therefore no formal evaluation process. I got a fairly good review after two years, but with no formal job duties, it was hard to figure out exactly what they wanted me to do. I was called the "CRM Manager," but they didn't have the faintest idea what CRM was, or what it mean to them, so that was an exercise in futility. The owner got suckered into buying a huge piece of custom software that was absolute crap, and was too bullheaded to admit his mistake after 4 million dollars of expense."

Would this gentleman be someone you'd want to bring in for an interview – or even sit next to on a train?

This person needs to go through the grieving process (yes, it's a big loss issue) before moving forward on a job search. So, if you find yourself in the angry or bitter stage, just give yourself some time to work through it before considering any interviews.

Being "laid off" or "RIF'd" (Reduction-in-Force) has been pretty common in the last few years, and is seen as a valid, not necessarily negative, reason for leaving a job. This is especially true if you were one of many:

"Was 1 of 19 salespeople laid off in a 70% reduction in force."

It is fine to mention this on a resume, but may be more appropriate in a cover letter, especially if you have lost your most recent position due to a RIF.

Quitting can be justified. In double income households, one spouse may need to quit for a relocation of the other.

A marriage to a co-worker sometimes necessitates a change. Quitting over a difference in business ethics can sometimes be valid.

Never use the word "Quit" as a reason for leaving. Here are some actual quotes from resumes where the authors specifically mentioned a reason for leaving:

"Reason for Change: Needed to return to U.S. to maintain resident alien status."

"Reason for Change: Father terminally ill in Canada. Moved to be closer to him."

"Reason for Change: Was offered a position with new career challenges in a major client company."

"Reason for Change: Western Regional manager requested that I head up new pilot program for Technical and Marketing support staff."

"Lack of funding for this start-up company forced a shut down of operations."

"Microsoft decided to enter our market by purchasing our company."

The "Silver Thread"

As an employer, or as a recruiter, I want to see some consistent thread in your career.

When you get a picture of what your consistent successes have been, you may need to look at your resume and your LinkedIn profile and thread this theme more obviously throughout.

I call this the Silver Thread. It will be the thread that subtly tells the reader what you want next, and links all your past experience together to logically prove you are ready and able for this next step.

For instance, I suggest that you provide a short description of each company on your resume. Thread your objective into these descriptions. There are at least a dozen ways to describe a company.

As an example, if you are best in a small, innovative, fast-growth start-up situation, but your resume lists large bureaucracies such as Dun & Bradstreet and Boeing, there is no thread.

However, a short description of the small innovative divisions within Dun & Bradstreet and Boeing Computer Services where you actually worked will link you to your potential in a small company.

For example:

"XYZ Company. A high-visibility $10MM VC-backed start-up software development division of Dun & Bradstreet.."

Again, in a job title description, you can weave your objective to become a Business Development or Turnaround Specialist:

"Recruited as VP Marketing to face the challenges of under-capitalization, a bootstrap operation, limited human resources, an embryonic marketplace, zero visibility, an out-of-the-mainstream platform, and lack of acceptance as a real application."

If your strengths lie in problem solving (as different from being the best Training Director in the world), list those accomplishments first. If your objective is to obtain the most lucrative commission plan in the industry, pepper your accomplishments with performance numbers.

A Reason for Leaving can also contain part of the silver thread of your objective. For example:

"Reason for Change: Saw the writing on the wall early on in the manufacturing industry, and made a decision to immerse myself in the emerging green technologies.."

And, if your thrill is setting up strategic partnerships, then name drop some of these that you have done. Name-dropping gives the employer a feel for the size and type of partnerships you are able to handle on their behalf.

The objective here is to tie all of your experience up with a bow in the spirit of uniqueness. Remember, the whole is the sum of its parts. You wouldn't be the great candidate you are today had it not been for all the successes and failures you've been through. Make them all count in the presentation of yourself in your resume, in your online profiles, and in your interviews.

CHAPTER 4

PROFILE

What is an online profile and why do I need one?

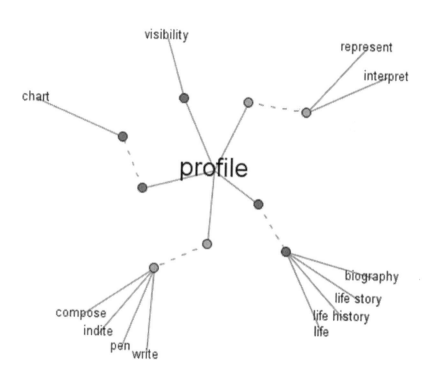

Now that you know exactly who you are, and what you bring to the table, where are employers going to find you?

Well... online.

Through the search engines and social networks and business groups and discussion forums.

I know, I know -- you never thought you'd stoop to Facebook at your level. Never say never. More in Chapter 7.

But you *must* get some sort of online profile out on the internet. Why?

Because the internet is where employers and recruiters look for job candidates now.

In the Introduction to this book, we discussed the fact that 83% of employers now use the web for their candidate searches instead of using job boards *and* instead of using outside recruiters.

A word about using external recruiters

Many employers now cut out the middlemen – headhunters – and teach their HR and recruiting staff to do their own search work internally, avoiding those huge fees.

It's important to make the distinction, then, between *external* recruiters (agencies and headhunters who charge fees to employers) and *internal* recruiters who are employees of hiring companies.

So that knee-jerk reaction of yesterday – *"I've lost my job so I must call a recruiter"* (the external kind) – may just be the most ineffective path to take for numerous reasons:

- Many employers have no budget for outside recruiter fees.

- Recruiters find job openings now the same way you can: on the internet.

- Recruiters are just as desperate for work as you are. They do not make money unless they fill a job opening. So, even though they have no fee contract with employers, they may send your resume to as many companies (and online job postings) as they can, hoping something will match. Once an external recruiter submits your resume to an employer, that company fears they are obligated to pay a fee, *and your resume is then put in the "do not engage" pile.*

- Employers are choosing to post their jobs on social networks now and not share them directly with headhunters for fees. Therefore you will be able to find more jobs yourself on the internet without going through headhunters.

How candidate selection is done

Here's how the search process now works inside company recruiting departments:

1. The internal recruiting staff members are directed to meet with hiring managers to create very detailed (Narrow and Deep) job descriptions that pinpoint the specific qualifications needed. *A sample job description is provided on the next page.*

2. The internal recruiter then examines the job description to identify relevant Keywords (see them in bold in the following job description).

3. The internal recruiter uses these (bolded) keywords in a Google or LinkedIn search to find online profiles (and resumes) that match those keywords.

Remember for later: the bolded keywords in the job description include:

Manufacturing
Director
Packaging
Pharmaceutical
Operations
Budget
Facility
SAP

Production
Process
Lean
Labor
Capital scorecard
Forecast
plant design
supply chain

Job Description for Director of Operations

The Director of Operations is responsible for ensuring that the firm's manufacturing network is positioned to be a source of competitive advantage and is capable of delivering the long term performance needed to support its business strategies. The **Director of Operations** will introduce **lean manufacturing** concepts to the organization and develop a program for continuous improvement; will represent Operations on **cross-functional teams** to support the development of **balanced scorecard metrics** and management reporting; will have responsibility for **capital projects**, the management of long and short term **production capacity planning** and capabilities, and overall production network **capacity analysis**. In this role you will:

- Evaluate current state manufacturing and **packaging** operations and provides key input into the company's strategic manufacturing plans, capacity and improvement strategies.
- Work closely with **Supply Chain** planning to study business demand and produce capacity utilization **forecasts** indicating **labor**, **equipment** and **facility requirements**.
- Work collaboratively with Operations, Supply Chain and **Logistics**, Administrative Functional Leaders and Executive Staff to identify areas of **waste elimination** and productivity improvement. Develop, improve and sustain productivity improvements using Lean **manufacturing disciplines**.
- Lead the deployment and improvement of problem solving skills at all levels based on Lean principles.

Requirements:
- At least 10 years experience in a leadership role in a **pharmaceutical** manufacturing environment, preferably **solid dosage** production.
- 5 + years actively participating in Lean development and execution across multiple plants
- Demonstrated successful experience leading and transforming organizations using Lean principles.
- Deep knowledge and understanding manufacturing and operations processes, tools and systems.
- Familiarity with **plant design** and **process flows**.
- **Budget** Preparation experience – Labor and capital.
- Working knowledge of Supply Chain Processes.
- Strong team leadership skills to lead, direct, and develop both plant and technical staff personnel. Strong track record of monitoring and developing leaders.
- Superior capability to engage technically and to influence cross-functionally.
- Advanced skills in problem analysis and problem solving in a manufacturing environment.
- Deep familiarity with the concepts of **Good Manufacturing Practices.**
- Experience with **SAP** is a plus

So let me show you how this keyword search works.

Using keywords to search for you

You don't really need to learn any of the jargon or syntax of the Google search strategies done by companies and recruiters. But you do need to know *what* they are looking for so that you can pack those ingredients into your resume and online profiles and even into the blog entries and articles you may write (more on that in Chapter 6).

Just for fun, let me show you a typical search that an internal recruiter would type into Google to find candidates for the Director of Operations Job Description on the previous page.

http://www.google.com/(intitle:~resume | inurl:~resume)
("manufacturing" | "director") (packaging | pharma | operations | budget |
facility| SAP | production | process | lean | labor | capital |scorecard
|forecast) ("plant design" | "supply chain" | "Good manufacturing") -~jobs
-apply -submit -eoe -template -example -sample

In about half a second, Google returns 98,200 results. The closest match to the combination of the keywords will come up first as in Figure 4-1 below.

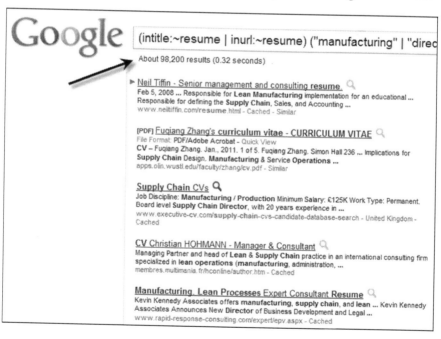

Figure 4-1

Then the internal recruiter would click on the "Neil Tiffin..." link and view his online profile to see if he is a fit. And so on with the others in this list (Well, actually, they'd look at just the first 2 pages of 98,200 results!)

So part of this Chapter is about sitting on the other side of the table from yourself -- trying to think from the company's side. What problems do they need solved? What keywords and phrases need to be on my resume and online profile in order for the company to find me? And how do I end up on the first 2 pages of search results like these folks did here?

Well, one way, as we just discussed, is to build an online profile, attach your resume to it, and populate both with lots of the keywords and phrases that employers would look for. Here's an example of a keyword-packed excerpt from one of the candidate resumes found through that Google search.

SUMMARY

Operations Management Professional with expertise in high-reliability systems manufacturing, **process flows, facility planning, logistics,** product management, advancing product quality, and managing **labor** and **capital budgets** in small and large **pharmaceutical** product and service businesses. Valued for the management of long and short term **production capacity planning** and capabilities and overall production network **capacity analysis.** Effectively employs a strong repertoire of **cross-functional** knowledge and skills to implement and deliver successful production and capacity **forecasts, management reporting, packaging** system integration and end-to-end customer satisfaction management in demanding **pharmaceutical manufacturing** environments.

CORE COMPETENCIES

Operations Management	Lean Manufacturing
Supply Chain Processes	Budget Planning and Forecasting
Plant Design and Analysis	Cross-Functional Team Leadership
Production & Process Flows	Quality Assurance / Continuous Improvement
Production Capacity Planning	Pharmaceutical Manufacturing

Remember the keyword list on page 59? You can see how this person's profile would be found and would float to the top of the search results list because of the close keyword match of his resume to the job description.

This is one piece of the keyword game in job search. You "customize" or "optimize" your resume for each job opening and pack it with the keywords from the job description so you'll appear near the top of the search results.

Other rules of the game include the strategic placement of those keywords within your documents and the ideal number of times they appear, but since this is not a detailed "how-to" manual, we won't include every trick here.

Not just Google

That same search for a Director of Operations can be done in many forums on the web.

As we've mentioned, LinkedIn is an online business network of more than 100 million people, and the basic membership is free. Individual business people can create a free LinkedIn profile and connect with others in their line of business and/or potential clients and/or potential employers.

Companies can also create a free LinkedIn profile page and invite interested parties to connect and be part of their online community, receiving direct messages, news updates, special product announcements and even job openings. In fact, the LinkedIn network is where employers and recruiters now look for all business candidates.

The LinkedIn people search

Employers log in to www.LinkedIn.com and go to the People field. There they fill in the keywords they are looking for in a candidate (like those bolded ones in the job description we just visited), and any geographic preferences, etc.

This particular search in my own network, for instance, yielded about 163 results for a Director of Operations with those skill keywords. If you notice below, I chose to sort the results by Keyword, so those that most closely match the keywords I entered will appear at the top of the list. See Figure 4-2 on the next page.

LinkedIn search for Director of Operations candidates

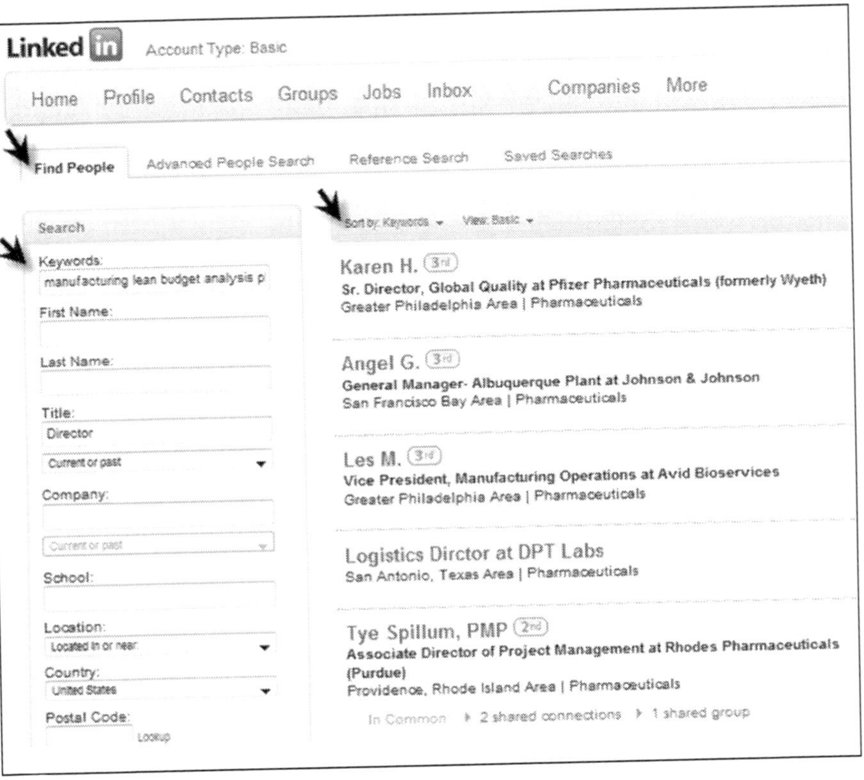

Figure 4-2

The other thing to note is the "level" designation to the right of each name. Most of these people are in my "3rd" degree network.

What's that?

If you know of the "Six Degrees Principle"[9], it's easier to understand.

---

[9] Some say that the LinkedIn concept is not rocket science but it *is* based on scientific theories of Information Routing Group (IRG) theory and Lateral Diffusion. **IRGs** are a component of social networks consisting of a semi-infinite set of similar interlocking and overlapping groups. Another related concept is **Lateral diffusion,** which is the process whereby information can be spread from one node in a social network to another, often in a selective way, and can rapidly traverse an entire population, but preferentially to those nodes likely to be interested, or needing to know. (Info from Wikipedia)

Six degrees of separation *(also referred to as the "Human Web") refers to the idea that everyone is on average approximately six steps away from any other person on Earth, so that a chain of, "a friend of a friend" statements can be made, on average, to connect any two people in six steps or fewer.*

You might want to refer back to the LinkedIn social network diagram in Chapter 1 (Figure 1-3) to remember how the "degrees" idea works.

Your LinkedIn network is comprised of:

1st degree contacts: your direct contacts whom you know.

2nd degree contacts: the contacts of those people in your 1st degree network (one level removed from you since you're just connected to those *through* someone else). You may or may not know them.

3rd degree contacts: the contacts of those people in your 2nd degree network

And the last level of connection is "all others" who show up last in any search.

For your purposes, think of LinkedIn and all social networking sites as avenues to get information out quickly (about yourself) to interested parties, and as tools to find information quickly for yourself (about people, jobs, companies, and industry topics).

And if LinkedIn isn't the original source where an employer finds you, they certainly will check LinkedIn to find out more about you, who you associate with, what people say about you, and how active you are in your industry.

If I receive a resume that simply has skills listed and a chronological history of job titles, I won't really know what you *know*.

So as an internal recruiter or hiring manager, I will look you up on the web (using Google or Yahoo or Bing and/or LinkedIn and Facebook and Twitter and Dogpile and White Pages and Zoominfo and Intelius and others discussed in later chapters) and see what is out on the internet about you.

Using these tools, I can find out:

- Your current home address, your former home address
- Your home phone number
- Relatives who are living with you
- Churches you attend
- Committees or School Boards or Condo Boards you have served on
- Political contributions you have made
- Speeches or presentations you have made
- Party or wedding pictures you are in
- Sports awards
- Mentions of your name in newspapers, magazines or books
- Articles you have written
- Photos you have posted
- Blog comments you have made
- Online advice you have given

And with this information, I can form an initial opinion about you, especially if I have your resume in front of me to aggregate all the data together.

This would be a good time to put down this book and go to your computer and "Google" yourself to see what comes up about you. Go to www.google.com and then type in your name in quotation marks, e.g. "George Felco."

So now that you're totally freaked out, remember that there is much you can do to control what's out there on the web about you. You can cause people to find things about you in the order that benefits *you*. You can follow the steps in this book to create and control your online profile and use it to proactively market your brand. While you are considering the Executive Program[10], you can get started right away with the approach that has been developed through our work with hundreds of candidates like you.

You need to be found, and it's important to steer people to the information you want them to see.

---

[10] The Executive Program at www.devonjames.com

Google

This would be a good time for a short Google lesson.

If you're familiar with the world of accounting, you'll know that LIFO means "last in, first out." With the internet, this phrase means that the most recent information about you on the web will appear at the top of the search results list when someone types in your name.

That's a simplification, since there are other Google rules we can teach you, but let's start with that concept.

So the most obvious way to control your online brand is to start stuffing good things about yourself into the worldwide web NOW and keep doing it. All that great data about you will rise to the top of the search results page, and will start pushing the old data down to pages three and four of the search results. People don't generally read past the second page of results when they look up something on Google, and so it is with employers and recruiters.

We'll get to the specifics about how to "stuff the web" like this, but first let's agree that you want searches for your name to come up with:

1) your LinkedIn Profile, (since you can control that content)
2) any Boards or Committees you've served on
3) any awards or patents or honors you've received
4) any brilliant comments you've made or answers you've contributed in your specialty discussion groups
5) any articles or papers you've written that relate specifically to your business body of knowledge

You do not want a search to come up with your address, your children's names, your divorce litigation, your ugly exit from a former employer, or a contentious email spat.

Building your online visibility

Visibility is not for the notoriety that is associated with Hollywood necessarily. It is all about getting found by searchers. It's a numbers game. You want to be visible to enough decision-makers so the likelihood of getting called for interviews increases.

Blogs

A blog ("web log") is simply a journal of comments about a certain topic contributed by anyone who wants to join the conversation. A blog is usually maintained by one person or company, and is parked out on the internet for access by anyone who wants to weigh in on the subject.

So which blog should you choose to participate in?

Start with something quick and easy that has immediate impact. Find blogs on your subject area and submit comments. Do this by going to Google (blogsearch.google.com) or to Bing or Yahoo and typing in the subject name e.g. "smart grid" plus the word "blog" if smart grid technology is one of your specialty areas.

Look through the list that comes up, scan a few of those blogs, and decide which ones you like (in attitude or discussion topics, for instance). Then dive in and add a comment to one of the conversations. You only have to write a sentence or two, like *"It is important to note that Biofuels had a flat year, with funding down by $200 million, which means...."*

And always "register" (they like to know who you are when making comments) in those blogs with your full name as it appears on your resume and on your LinkedIn profile. (It's free, by the way.)

The search engines (Google, Yahoo, Bing, etc) will see your comment with your name attached to it and "index" it. Then, when an employer or recruiter searches online for a candidate who knows, Smart Grid and Biofuels, your name will show up in their search results.

This is why your chosen keywords and keyword phrases are so important. Be sure to use them in your online conversations and comments. You are building (and controlling) your brand! You are "seeding" the internet with the content you want displayed when someone searches on a topic and/or searches on your name.

Choose a few blogs, and make comments on them every few days. It's just like giving advice to employees who walk into your office every day with issues. Or compare it to a short management meeting called to discuss a particular issue. Weigh in. Get heard. Get found on the internet more quickly.

More on blogging in Chapter 8 when we discuss your targeting of preferred employers.

Google profile

Next, create a Google profile. This will get you "found" if someone just does a simple search on your name in Google. Even though you know that people won't be searching for you by name until you're a candidate, it's good to have another profile on the internet *that you control*. Besides, the Google bird feeds its own nest first.

Google (www.google.com/profiles) will walk you through the process. See Figure 4-3.

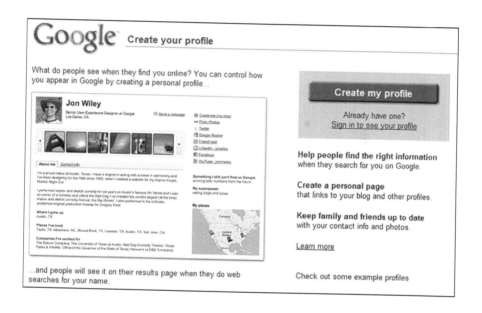

Figure 4-3

LinkedIn profile

Go to www.linkedin.com and sign in to create a profile. It's free. And here is the official learning center published by LinkedIn: http://learn.linkedin.com/

I'll let you in on some not-so-obvious LinkedIn secrets here.

1. You must have a photo on your LinkedIn Profile. The consensus is that if you don't like the way you look, neither will we.

2. You should name your photo like so: Fname_Lname_specialty_title. For instance, Robert_Miller_Tax_Specialist_Finance_CFO. This is because Google indexes images and the more content you have out on the web that you can control, the easier it is for you to manipulate who finds you and what they find.

3. Your professional headline should be similarly "function-titled" as in Figure 4-3, instead of your current title. Few will search for "consultant" or "true leader and ethical businessman." No joke, I've seen that.

4. You need to have at least 500 connections in order to show up on the searches that the recruiters are doing. Statistically, if you have fewer than 100 connections, the result will be that fewer than 3% of the 60 million people on LinkedIn will be able to see you.

5. You need to join at least 5 Groups in your area of interest or industry specialty. It is important for a few reasons:
    a. It shows that you are active in your specialty area
    b. It shows that you are connected to similar professionals as useful resources and sources of up-to-date information
    c. You will find jobs discussed in the Groups and their sub-groups that are NOT posted in the regular LinkedIn Jobs.
    d. You will find discussions about problems that you can solve for companies.
    e. You can use the discussion forums to increase your visibility by adding short comments or helpful suggestions within the specialty groups. This will get you noticed and will further your brand as an authority with Google for that subject area.

6. You need at least one recommendation for every job in the past 10 years, with a minimum of 6 total recommendations. Many employers will not even consider candidates who have no recommendations on their profile.
    Note: Your recommendations should not be reciprocal. It dilutes their credibility if I look on the profiles of everyone you've recommended and they are the only ones who have recommended you back as a favor.

7. Under the "Specialty" section, just list a string of keywords instead of making complete sentences. These keywords must be the words an employer would search for to find you. More on keywords a bit later.

8. Don't wait to populate and enhance your LinkedIn profile. Once you are thinking of looking for new opportunities, it becomes too apparent if you suddenly are joining Groups and inviting connections like mad. Yesterday I received an alert in my network that a gentleman had just joined 37 groups on New Years Day. Either it was a New Year's resolution, or he was suddenly looking for an instant network to help him in his job search. Desperation with "instant friends" never works.

9. Find specific recruiters within LinkedIn who specialize in your niche and invite them to connect with you. But do NOT ask them for help in your job search. (Remember the discussion about recruiters in Chapter 4.) They will look at your profile when they get your LinkedIn invitation. If you're a match to any of their fee assignments, of course they will contact you. You don't need to remind them to do that. It's money in their pockets. Otherwise, they have no use for you. But you have use for them. Simply having vastly-connected recruiters in your social network will increase your visibility very quickly, and get you "found" on more searches.

10. Using a file sharing application like Box.net (found on your LinkedIn page), upload your resume onto your Profile page. This gives Google a double dose of your keywords since both your resume and profile are in the same place, and you also provide a "one-stop-shop" for recruiters. Just remember to take off your address and phone numbers before you post your resume for your network to see.

Something to keep in mind: The more times you use a specific keyword in your resume and/or your LinkedIn Profile, the higher you rank in Google for that subject area. However, Google also is not stupid, so don't try to game the system by going overboard.

Let's talk again about SEO (search engine optimization) as it relates to "optimizing" your LinkedIn profile. This "SEO" concept is not exclusive to Google. You want to "optimize" your LinkedIn profile so that other LinkedIn users will find you. Just as on your resume, you do need keywords. But you also need your endorsers – those who give you a good recommendation on your LinkedIn page – use those keywords if they will. And be mindful of the names of the LinkedIn Groups that you join. For instance, if you had to choose between joining a Group called "Smart Grid Executives" or "Save Our Planet," you probably should choose the former.

LinkedIn "degrees"

If you are in my 1st or 2nd degree network on LinkedIn (in other words, I am linked directly to you or to someone you know) then when I search for a keyword that is in your profile, you are going to show up on my first list of "hits" in the LinkedIn universe. If you *are* on LinkedIn, but *not in my network*, you will show up on one of the last pages of results with no last name when I search for you, and guess what? I never get to the last pages of the results. I always get to the first few pages.

For instance, I did a LinkedIn search for a CFO near Seattle with the keywords of "executive" and "finance" in their profiles. This search returned 240 people in my network who match. You can see this below in Figure 4-4. Those who are my 1st degree connections will come up first.

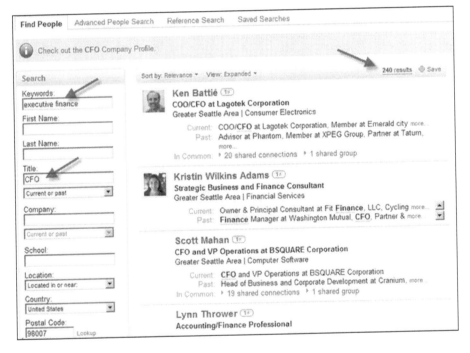

Figure 4-4

The other high visibility drivers (blogging, group discussions, articles and answers) are crucial as well, and we'll take all of Chapter 6 to walk you through those pieces of your online presence.

The newest tools for profiling yourself

As an executive job seeker, you still want to "just get in front of the CEO" for that interview. But hopefully after reading Chapters 1-4 you've bought into the fact that you first need all your modern ducks in a row. And now that you've lined them all up, there is an urge to do a loud-quacking wing-flapping dive bomb on those CEOs, armed with all your documentation...

Well, actually you can.

Technology has brought the internet into the forefront of most search activity in the business world. It also has advanced so quickly that many technologies are able to converge and offer spectacular efficiencies not possible before.

One of the sectors where this convergence is well-suited is the employment arena. And it's high time technology takes a value-added role in this market. You would have thought that the emergence of online resume databases back in the 80s would fix the problems of matching candidates to jobs.

In fact, the opposite happened.

Since any person could electronically apply for any job, the corporate hiring system became completely bogged down in applicant volume for every job opening.

Then came the software that would assess the personalities of job seekers and magically predict their match to a job. When that pill was found to remedy only one piece of the qualifying process, several new technology products emerged to help fill in the screening gap. Some guaranteed an "artificial intelligence" solution, some offered the salve of semantic web tools, and still others developed magical ranking software that will produce the matching candidate list from hundreds of applicants.

Today, HR and recruiting departments, with their 10-year junkyard of screening tools strewn about, are even more burdened by the overwhelming number of job seekers. The hiring process has not shortened over the years. In fact it has been regulated and automated and tabulated so much that even the most dedicated and well-meaning internal recruiters often are too buried to make truly informed screening decisions.

Multi-media strategy

What you want is to "get in front of the hiring manager," right? You figure that a resume is only one small data point about you. You know that you could communicate your uniqueness and value if you had a chance to talk to him. Well, if you can't do that in person, use technology.

Find a tool (we have one for you) that aggregates all your information onto one screen, including a professional video interview that presents you speaking peer-to-peer about your industry, and then deliver it to the hiring manager over email.

Here's the strategy behind these newest multi-media presentation tools.

The trend today is to give a little entertainment in return for someone's attention. This is not to say that your resume, profile, and video are entertaining. The idea is to give short bursts of information-rich communication that are respectful of the viewer's time. These bursts, or pitches as we call them, must be valuable to the recipient in some way. So again, it must be about *them* instead of just a sales pitch about something that *you* want.

When you send focused and relevant data to a C-level decision maker, you are showing him a high level of respect for his time. You are also making the message about *him* (e.g. about a targeted market you could capture *for him*, or a targeted problem you could solve *for him*.)

InterviewStudio

One of the platforms we have developed for you is called InterviewStudio. It is an aggregation of all your information onto one screen, as shown in Figure 4-5. It is a "showcase" of your total asset value as a skilled executive and as a corporate culture fit. (You can visit the "bit.ly" link above Figure 4-5 to view an actual showcase).

We create one of these showcases for you in the Executive Program, but the InterviewStudio product is available to anyone who wants to create one to send to employers. Either way, you might want to consider having one for the Pitch process described in Chapter 10.

Blake Cahill's InterviewStudio Showcase
http://bit.ly/CahillShowcase

Figure 4-5

Note that this "showcase" includes all your assets, including:

- that resume you spent so much time on
- your LinkedIn and Google profiles accessed by the buttons at the top
- the recommendations from your connections
- the results of that assessment test you took
- a video interview which we produce and edit for you
- portfolio documents or reviews or cover letters or awards
- links to your website or online articles

Your showcase is the all-inclusive profile that you can email to your choice of contacts. See this URL link? This is what you would email to your contacts.

http://www.interviewstudio.com/show/Thaddeus/Gunn/18

Oh, and go ahead and view this one too if you'd like! He has a very interesting answer to the question "Tell me 10 ways to use a pencil other than writing."

This type of multi-media showcase simulates an entire first interview and gets right to the heart of the matter: Do they want to bring you in to talk further or not?

Essentially you are *doing all the due diligence upfront for the employer*, so that your candidacy can move forward more quickly than others.

The hiring manager can see you and hear you in the stored video at the same time as they are viewing your other profile documents. You are coming across as a "human capital asset" not as just keywords on paper... and not in some form of notes from a third party.

You are actually going through a first interview as the passionate problem-solver that you are. Since you've been coached through this video-taped interview (by us or by another professional of your choice), and you've put some real effort into communicating your true asset value, a huge part of the "selling" work is done.

Think of it like this: If they call you for a live in-person interview *after* they've viewed your InterviewStudio showcase, half the battle is over. They already know a lot about you and still like you! (...joke)

Once you've put together a showcase like the one above, you have another "branding" tool that you control, and that you can include as a link in your resume, your LinkedIn profile, your Tweets, your Facebook page, and in your cover letters and even in your email signature line.

Your email signature would look something like this:

```
Michael Sweeney
Vice President, Worldwide Sales
XYZ Corporation
www.xyzcorp.com
425.555.1212
http://www.linkedin.com/in/michaelsweeney

Interview
  STUDIO http://www.interviewstudio.com/show/MichaelSweeney
```

In chapters 9 and 10 we'll show you how and when to push your entire set of profile information out to targeted employers, recruiters, hiring managers, and industry influencers.

CHAPTER 5

CONNECT

How and Why to increase your business connections quickly

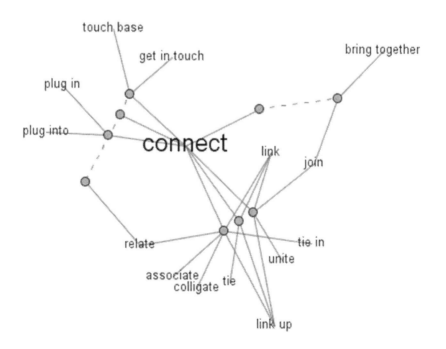

Now that you've constructed your resume, your LinkedIn profile and your InterviewStudio showcase, how do you use these to get a job?

Executive recruiters

The old way to get an executive job was to "send out the word" to former colleagues and to the major executive search firms... mostly in the form of phone calls or sending them resumes. Right?

Within those search firms, you would be catalogued as "available" and most likely would get a call from them for more information. At the time, you thought that call was because they were impressed with your background and they might have a current client who could employ you. Sometimes that was true... especially back in the 90s when every company was growing and hiring.

What you didn't know was that you were simply helping us (search firms) to build our networks. We would ask you enough questions to make you feel we were interested in you, but we would sneak in these questions as well:

"Where are you currently interviewing?" (Then as soon as we hung up with you, we would call that company to offer our headhunting services to them and maybe even send over a resume of one of our other candidates.)

"Who did you interview with there?" (Under the guise of "I might know someone in that company who could help get you get further along the hiring process there" we were really getting the direct contact from you to shoot over another candidate's resume for whom we would be paid a fee.) Seriously. Why would we help you get that job if we wouldn't make any money off that transaction?

"What other employers would you like us to introduce you to?" (Here you are making our job much easier as you have researched other employers for us and may even know of their current openings.)

We would then do an immediate calling campaign to the top 10 employers in your niche market saying that we "have direct contacts with the executive team at [your company name] and have insider information that some of them may be leaving soon and would they [the competitor companies] be interested in these under-the-radar, hard-to-find executives?"

So, social business networking - and the race to be more connected than the next person - has been around a long time.

Connecting today

Here's what's different now:

- About 80%[11] of the traditional recruiters who still work as we just described are being cut out of the process now. *You don't need them to get directly in front of the right people.* You can research companies yourself online. You can find job openings online. You can introduce yourself online. You can converse with hiring managers directly online.

- The internal recruiters of most employers are now doing all their searching for *you* on the internet. Many employers have also stopped using external search firms now that they have discovered the world of online search. So your job now is not only to create a detailed profile of yourself, but to place that profile in strategic places where you're sure to be found by employers searching for the experts they wish to hire.

So how do you get your profile directly in front of employers and their recruiters?

You use the "connections" features in these online networks. You search for people on LinkedIn and Facebook and other online social networks (see Chapters 8 and 9) and simply hit a "connect" button, and wait for them to accept your invitation to connect (a few minutes, or hours). *You're now "in" their network. That profile you slaved over will appear in their searches now if you have the right keywords in your resume and profile.* Refer back to Chapters 3 and 4.

For instance, you'll start growing your LinkedIn network by finding a few people you already know, and asking them to join your network. That's fine.

---

[11] There will always be a number of professional retained recruiters who add value to employers and candidates for the whole-person matching, but the "keyword matching" recruiters who charge traditional fees are being replaced by social media staff inside informed employers.

But if you're looking for a job, you'll want to expand your network to include strategic decision-makers within companies you might like to join.

Here's how.

Go to the search field at the top of your LinkedIn page (as in Figure 5-1), select the "Companies" dropdown and type in a few keywords. Here we used "transportation OR maritime OR logistics" just to find operating companies in these industries.

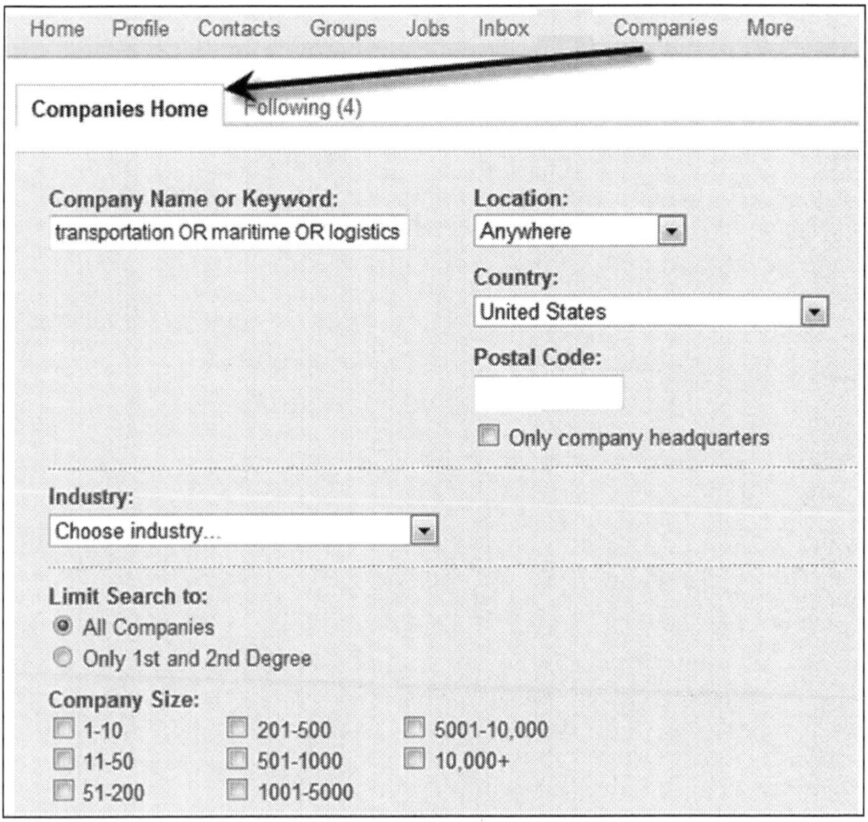

Figure 5-1

This Company Search on LinkedIn resulted in 311 companies found. As a bonus, you can see the number of job openings in each company on the same screen (Figure 5-2).

Company Search on LinkedIn

	Company	Headquarters	Employees
1st	**Walmart** (3 jobs)	Fayetteville, Arkansas Area	2,000,000
1st	**HCL Technologies** (4 jobs)	Noida Area, India	10,000+
1st	**Pacific Gas and Electric Company** (11 jobs)	San Francisco Bay Area	20,000
1st	**URS Corporation** (4 jobs)	San Francisco Bay Area	50,000
1st	**VanceInfo** (1 job)	London, United Kingdom	10,000+
1st	**General Motors** (7 jobs)	Greater Detroit Area	10,000+
1st	**JDA Software** (4 jobs)	Phoenix, Arizona Area	1001-5000
1st	**SunGard Availability Services** (12 jobs)	Greater Philadelphia Area	1001-5000
1st	**Ascentium** (3 jobs)	Greater Seattle Area	500
2nd	**Cathay Pacific Airways** (1 job)	Amsterdam Area, Netherlands	21,000
2nd	**Touchstone Wireless** (1 job)	Greater Philadelphia Area	2,000
2nd	**Trimac Transportation** (6 jobs)	Calgary, Canada Area	2,500

311 results found. Keywords: transportation OR maritime OR logistics Hiring on LinkedIn
1st – You know someone at company   2nd – Your connection(s) know someone at company

Figure 5-2

You can now click on the name of the company in Figure 5-2 which will take you to a LinkedIn "company" page.

We clicked on "Pacific Gas and Electric Company" (PG&E). They have 11 jobs open so we want to see who we should connect to within the company to get on their radar and end up in their searches.

Here's the key... the PG&E LinkedIn page also tells you they have 5,329 employees profiled on LinkedIn (Figure 5-3).

Figure 5-3

So click on that link to their employees and browse through them.

Oh, look who's on LinkedIn... their very-well-connected internal recruiter, Michael Holland. See Figure 5-4. If you want to be found for any jobs inside PG&E, you would want to be in Michael's network so you'll come up in his keyword searches for candidates with your skills.

Michael Holland, Staffing Professional at PG&E

Figure 5-4

But how do you connect with targeted people you don't know?

Groups

Go back to Michael's LinkedIn profile and you'll see that he is a member of these Groups and others:

- BANG – Bay Area Networking Group
- Complete Career Network
- Facebook User Group
- Global Energy Professionals
- Global Petroleum Forum

Go join these Groups or at least one of them, and you will both be a member of the same Group(s). Then LinkedIn lets you connect directly with him through that Group online (Figure 5-5) without having to know his contact information:

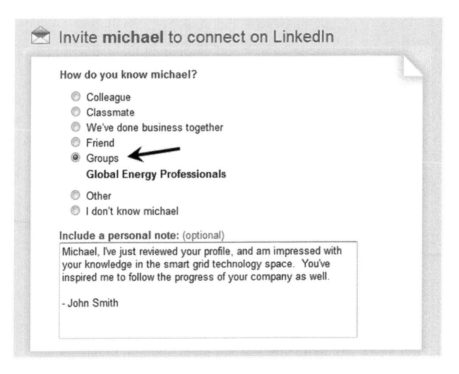

Figure 5-5

In the Executive Program, we work with executives to increase their online virtual networks by finding and adding specific valuable connections. Readers of this book, right away, can try out what was just described about LinkedIn. Undoubtedly, you'll find people in these companies whom you forgot you even knew! They will become 1st degree contacts in your network.

Now, remember that one of the goals in having a LinkedIn profile is to appear on as many radars as possible. This means being officially connected to many people in LinkedIn and/or in Facebook and BranchOut (See Chapter 7).

It's pretty simple math. To appear on the radar of 10,000 people, you need to be either:

- directly connected to 10,000 people; or
- directly connected to 500 people who each have 20 connections themselves; or
- directly connected to 100 people who each have 1000 connections.

Since it takes time to connect directly with people one at a time, it only makes sense to have your online communities do some of that connection work for you. So try to connect with those people who have a lot of connections themselves.... and who are in your area of interest/business of course.

It's the same logic as using Television (or the internet) to get the news out to the world instead of delivering a newspaper to every household every day.

Following and subscribing

Remember that you're trying not only to connect to people, but the ultimate goal is to connect to opportunities – chances for gainful employment for instance. So you also want to "connect" to companies and to events and educational sites to keep yourself *in the know*.

An often overlooked tool for this is the "Follow" feature.

Let's use PG&E again for an example. Note in Figure 5-6 that most Company pages have a "Follow Company" button. This means that you will receive notices every time that company posts something new to their profile.

The "Follow Company" button

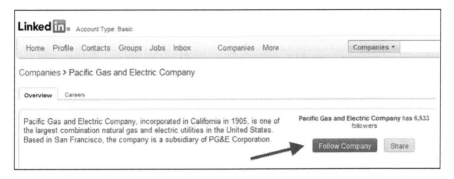

Figure 5-6

One of the significant things about the Follow function is that the company you are following will see that you are following and will know that you are interested in them as a company.

Extend that thought. When you "Follow" a person, it is a compliment. You are saying that you think their comments are worthy of note, and that you'd like to receive all their comments without having to go online and look for them.

On most online discussions, posts are formatted with the name and photo of the commenter, and a link for those who wish to follow them, like this:

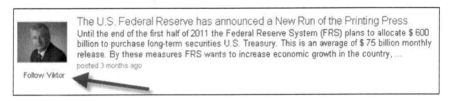

You can choose to follow someone for a number of reasons, but keep in mind, in your job search, you will want to follow people who can give you valuable information about a company, or who can lead to the introduction of an opportunity.

It stands to reason that you'd want to follow and connect with high-level influential people.

In fact, it is becoming quite trendy for CEOs to blog. Last year in MarketBeat, The Wall Street Journal[12] listed some of the top CEO blogs:

- Jonathan Schwartz, "Jonathan's Blog" — CEO of Sun Microsystems
- Bill Marriott, "On the Move" — CEO of Marriott International
- Mike Critelli, "Open Mike" — executive chairman of Pitney Bowes
- Robert Lutz, "Fast Lane" — GM vice chairman
- Michael Hyatt, "From Where I Sit" — CEO of Thomas Nelson Publishers

So if you're interested in working for one of these companies, you should follow the company blog, and even their CEO's blog, to get a feel for the corporate culture, mission, and the latest news from the top, as found in the Marriott blog.

Figure 5-7

---

[12] WSJ February 13, 2011 MarketBeat
http://blogs.wsj.com/marketbeat/2007/07/12/the-ceo-blogs/

Bill Marriott blogs not only about personal things, but about employment, diversity, and the environment. You'll get a good feel about the company message and mission from following him.

In this blog there is no "Follow" button, but there is a "Subscribe" field, which accomplishes the same thing.

Profile

I'm Bill Marriott, Chairman & CEO of Marriott International.

Email Alert
To receive new posts, enter your email address

Subscribe

The point is to follow people and/or subscribe to the blogs of those who are connected to your industry. They will not necessarily connect you to a job. It is up to *you* to follow the news and the connection trails to find or even to create opportunities.

We'll talk more about the power of following and subscribing later in chapter 7.

CHAPTER 6

Contribute

You're a niche authority. Get your knowledge noticed.

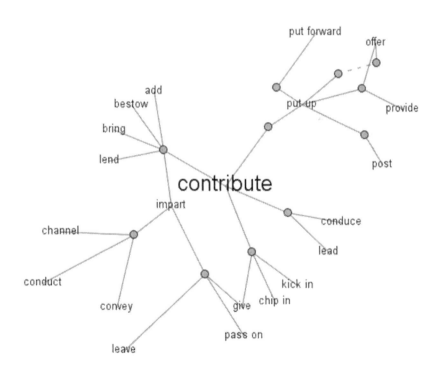

You're a niche authority

You *are* an authority in your areas of experience. You *are* very knowledgeable on some Narrow and Deep topics. But you can't wait "until the interview" or "until the reference checking stage" for an employer to verify that. You may not even get that far unless they can look around on the internet and find some validation of your expertise.

In this chapter, you'll see how important it is not only to be *found*, but more importantly, to be considered as a strong candidate – an expert – in your field.

Remember that employers are looking for experts to solve their specific problems. If you hope to get the attention of a company, or even a retained recruiter, regarding a particular job, you must be a very close match to their specific needs.

And it's not about YOU

Matching yourself up to jobs is not about *you*. Sitting in a job interview is not about *you*. It is all about what you can do for *them*.

This is a hard pill to swallow for many of our clients, but it is true. Remember our discussion in Chapter 1 about defining your strengths, and determining the specific areas where you can solve *their* business problems? To repeat, this is mandatory for four reasons:

- Employers have reduced headcount but are trying to produce the same amount of output, and many issues have been left to fix "when the economy comes back." So *when and if* they hire a new employee, that person had better be valuable immediately. They don't have time or money to waste on a bad hire.

- Not only is there an overabundance of great unemployed talent on the market in the U.S. right now, but globalization has opened up a whole new toolbox of available talent as well. Their global experience gives these candidates some advantages in that they may have solved problems in their economies that we haven't faced yet. Further, since their countries may be smaller and closer geographically, they bring cross-border trade knowledge that you may not have.

- The playbook has been re-written. Technology has never stopped moving forward, and now many positions require new skill sets - internet search expertise, culture sensitivity, international business experience, mobile communications savvy, and an entirely new methodology of marketing and commerce driven by technology. You have to prove that you have kept up with globalization, and the technologies that your next employer will need.

- Harvard Business Review (HBR)[13] phrases this last point the best: *High performance companies need up-and-comers who can grow a new business, not just manage an old one. Long before successful business hits its revenue peak, the basis of competition on which it was founded expires. [Therefore they need...] high performers who turn conventional wisdom on its head and ... focus on fixing what doesn't yet appear to be broken... [those who...] see [hidden] changes in customer needs and create the next basis of competition in their industry.*

To summarize, we're talking about what it means to be the most valuable candidate to your next employer – in a decade of stiff competition.

Some of you "senior" readers will be shaking your head at point 4 above. Be sure to read about age discrimination – and what is mistaken for age discrimination – in Chapter 10.

Touch points of due diligence about you

Proving that you are the best person for the job *is no longer done in the interview.* I can't stress that enough. Today interviews are for final validation of your corporate culture match, your poise and attitude, your communications skills, and your thinking style.

The first opinion of the employer about your value is formed long before you ever are invited in for an interview. Your resume is just one of many sources of information about you. Unfortunately your readers [screeners, HR, recruiters, and hiring managers] have become jaded over the years about the credibility of those documents.

---

[13] Harvard Business Review, January-February 2011, page 83 in the article "Reinvent Your Business Before It's Too Late" by Paul Nunes and Tim Breene

To my point, there are hundreds of professional resume writers and online resume templates that can make an aerobics instructor look like the world's best Director of Special Events.

Today, employers and recruiters use a combination of touch points to research your accomplishments, your popularity, your personality fit, your writing skills, your community involvement, etc. – upfront – before they decide whether you're worth an interview.

- Google
- LinkedIn
- Zoominfo
- Glassdoor
- Hoovers
- Facebook
- LinkedIn Group Discussions
- LinkedIn Answers
- Yahoo Answers
- eZineArticles
- Wikipedia
- Ask.com
- Industry niche Blogs

Potential employers simply type in your name to see what they can find – where you've been quoted, the articles you've written or questions you've answered online. They're looking for how your brain works, what your tone is, and if your opinions will add value to their team. This is in addition to the data they've found on you regarding location, friend networks, community work, etc. (discussed in Chapter 1).

So it's *your* responsibility to do these searches on yourself before the employers do, and then launch some activity to:

- create your brand (if you find nothing about your name out there!);
- change your brand (if you find irrelevant references to your name, or some embarrassing quote, or even digital dirt);
- control your brand (consistently monitor what's out there about you).

Reputation Management

The exercise of "contributing" information on the internet is a large part of controlling your brand, which is also called Reputation Management. This is another step you must take to ensure that anyone who finds your name will be presented with true and positive information about you.

Today there are vendors who specialize in cleaning up your online brand and monitoring it for you going forward. If you're not participating in our Executive Program yet, you might want to look into paying for a service like this (e.g. www.Reputation.com).

So, let's talk about the specifics of "talking your way to a clean brand."

There are public website forums (no registration required) where you can enter a comment or contribute an answer about topics in your areas of specialty. In fact, it's no coincidence that we just listed them above as the sites where employers look. (Duh. You need to be on the roster and suited up if you want to be called in to play.)

We'll discuss a few of these sites in this chapter.

Here's an important branding note about your name. Always use your real name when contributing comments and answers. And by "real name" I mean the name you have displayed on your resume and on your LinkedIn profile.

Why?

Because every time something new appears on the internet with your name on it (contributed by you or by others), that activity gets indexed out on the web.

When people search for your name in Google or Bing or Yahoo, the latest references to your name will appear in the results list. Hence, you want to start taking control of where and how your name appears.

So let's see how this is done.

Group discussions

First let's use LinkedIn Discussions.   If you're near a computer, you might want to log in and experiment with the LinkedIn Groups as you read this.

We talked about LinkedIn in Chapter 4 as a place to join relevant industry Groups and enjoy the benefits of a) being able to easily connect with those Group members, b) posturing yourself as worthy of membership, and c) participation in Group discussions on topics that you know well.

One note about Groups: There are "Open" Groups (open to anyone to join) and there are "Members Only" Groups (also called "closed groups" -- you have to be invited in or approved to join once you request membership).

What difference does it make to you?

A couple of things are relevant here.

- Google doesn't see or "index" the discussions in the closed or "members only" Groups. This means that employers wouldn't see what you have said if they looked up your name to do research on you and you had only participated in closed Groups.

  There is a big upside to closed Groups. Only the Group's members see your discussions and they may be enough of a target audience to get you noticed for your Narrow and Deep specialty.   After all, your Group may already contain the only people you need to be noticed by. For instance, if you are a orthopedic surgeon and you join a membership Group of your peers, you may have joined specifically to discuss the pros and cons of using a new robotic device.   You may not want the world to participate in or observe these conversations, but you do want to converse intelligently with your peers about topics of shared expertise.

  For example, I've joined a LinkedIn Group called CEO Network. See Figure 6-1 on the next page. It is a closed "members only" group. At this writing there are only 313 members. I like this Group because it is small and under-the-radar. I can discuss business issues freely with C-level executives and neither of us have to worry about our discussions getting picked up by Google.

Closed Group example

Figure 6-1

- On the other hand, if your primary goal in participating in discussions about your industry is to appear in as many candidate searches as you can, then you want to join the Open Groups. Google does index the discussions in those LinkedIn Groups, and you can drive your "authority index" to the top of the charts with consistent participation and keyword density.

Now, notice in Figure 6-1 that you can either start a new discussion on a topic you want to introduce to the Group (Open or Members Only) *or* you can comment on someone else's discussion (easier).

For example, if you're going into a meeting regarding China trade strategy, you might want to read a peer-group discussion to see what's new or to ask a question of your constituents.

All you need to do to read *or* to ask a question in the Group discussion is to click the Comment tab, shown by the arrow in Figure 6-1, and type in a few sentences of comment.

Since our discussion topic is "Getting Your China Strategy Right" your comment could be a question about a strategy or a suggestion for a new strategy. Now, if your comment is "Strategy, Schmmategy... money talks...," I'd be tempted to brand you as a cynic, a poor man or an Econ professor...or all three...

So be aware of your brand when making comments. Especially if this were an Open Group. Bam! Google would pick up that comment attached to your name and now you're indexed on the internet with your name plus that Group name plus your comment's words.

So make sure your comments are not knee-jerk or uninformed, and for goodness sake try not to use the word "Schmmategy."

SEO (Search Engine Optimization)

OK, switch hats for a moment.

Let's say you're an *employer* looking for a job candidate who knows a lot about global transportation issues.

You go to www.google.com and type in "transportation issues in China" since you want to find someone who is an expert on this topic. The results of your search are in Figure 6-2.

Results of search: "transportation issues in China"

Figure 6-2

Google found 36,600,000 instances out on the web where this topic was discussed.

So how the heck did this guy Martin Rowe come up *first* in the list of 36.6 million???

It's complicated. But it's not rocket science.

Notice in Figure 6-3 that Martin Rowe has his own website, has a LinkedIn profile, has spoken and written about the China transportation topic in several places *and* the media reprints and reuses his comments in additional articles.

WOW.

Figure 6-3

This all has to do with industry phraseology like "Search Engine Optimization" (SEO) of his website, and "Keyword Density" of his online profiles and "Ranking" by Google of the sheer volume of his name occurrences.

You can spend time learning and applying these techniques (SEO, Keyword Density, and Ranking), but I would venture to say that your time would be better spent writing an article in your area of expertise, or preparing a video interview to send out.

A few professional firms in the employment field have fine tuned the use of these technologies and can produce results more quickly and comprehensively than you might if you are new to this process. The Devon James Executive Job Search Program specializes in just that: elevating our participants' presence within search results.

So, although it's not necessary for you to jump into the deep dive technology of these techniques, it *is* important to understand the logic of how to control your brand and quickly appear as the expert that you are.

For example, you don't have to be a world-renowned expert, or write a book, or get on a speaking tour, or obtain a patent, or appear on Oprah to be considered an authority in your area of expertise. You just have to prove your expertise by participating in relevant online discussions and by contributing answers to industry questions.

The more your-name-plus-those-industry-keywords are found together on the web, the higher you will be on the internet "list" for that subject matter.

Where to contribute

The days of printed encyclopedias, dictionaries, thesauruses, and other reference books are slowly fading into history. The internet has all of this content online to be searched using keywords. We no longer tell our children to "go look it up"… We tell them to "Google it."

And actually, to augment Google, Bing and Yahoo, many of us are turning to sites where we can ask questions in an unstructured way -- much easier than trying to guess the most relevant keyword on the subject.

For example, "What are the newest energy resources available in the U.S.?"

Figure 6-4 on the next page shows the first five results provided by Google in answer to that question..

Notice that the top 3 are *paid* advertisements. You certainly don't want to pay for a listing to be noticed on Google.

The 4th in the list is an article from a popular magazine, and unless you are the Martin Rowe type, it will take awhile to get that kind of press in well-known publications.

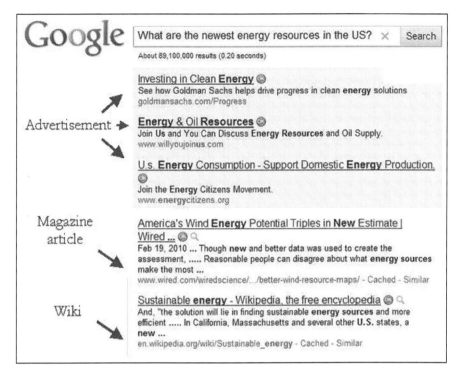

Figure 6-4

But notice that the 5th highest result (out of 89,100,000) is from Wikipedia, the largest online encyclopedia in the world.

There is a place for *you* on Wikipedia. Yes, *you* can contribute *your* knowledge to Wikipedia[14] and ride the coattails of its high volume of traffic. Here are the Wikipedia options for doing so (from their website... see footnote):

- Respond to a <u>request for comment</u> or provide a <u>third opinion</u>;
- Give a requested <u>editor review</u>;
- <u>Peer review</u> or give <u>feedback</u> on some articles;
- Comment at <u>Featured portal candidates</u> and <u>Portals at peer review</u>;
- Make recommendations on articles listed at <u>Good article reassessment</u>;
- Respond to the <u>Reward board</u> or <u>Bounty board</u>.

---

[14] From the Wikipedia site: http://en.wikipedia.org/wiki/Wikipedia:Community_portal#Todo

If you're reading this book in print and not on a digital device, it's difficult to determine exactly what these options are from just this list, but you can go to the Wikipedia website and see if any of these activities strike a chord with you.

The point is that if you contribute comments on high traffic sites, you earn higher "authority points" so to speak.

On page 94, we listed several popular sites where people look for *online* answers. Wikipedia was just one of them.

Of that list, pay particular attention to high traffic sites when you have a lot to say about a topic (as opposed to an occasional comment), especially these:

Yahoo Answers
Ask.com
LinkedIn Answers
Wikipedia and their Answers.com (see how highly they ranked in Figure 6-2)

High traffic means that a lot of people go to the site for information. In other words, if you hang around there, you will get noticed. Your consistent and keyword-laden comments and advice will rank you high on the list when an employer searches your topic of expertise. So, the importance of *where* you discuss things cannot be overstated.

Said another way, if you participate in a discussion Group with very few members and very low activity, then it doesn't get you a lot of broad visibility. Again, Google likes high-traffic sites.

These sites cover a broad range of subjects and anyone can register to ask questions and/or contribute answers. For instance, you would go to www.ask.com and search for questions in your specialty area that you could answer with some authority. Your answers would be visible publicly. And of course they would be picked up by Google immediately and added to the growing number of instances where you appear online.

It's worth pausing for a moment to reflect on how the global knowledge base of almost every subject on the planet has morphed. Not only is there more data available to more people because of the internet, but the source of information can now come from anyone. *You* are the new Merriam Webster.

The new Mr. Britannica. The new Funk & Wagnall. You and others like you are the creators, editors, monitors of the new world bank of knowledge.

You can define concepts and products online, have your writing approved, and it becomes part of the new world library in the sky.

OK, back down to earth.

Choosing where to post a comment

I just went to www.wiki.answers.com and typed in a question about smart grid technology. If you're in the energy field, you might want to do this search yourself right now. There are at least 3 unanswered questions there waiting for you, including:

What makes the smart grid smart? | Unanswered
What are going to be the 2011 free agents? | Unanswered
What industries use smart materials? | Unanswered

What a great opportunity for you to showcase your expertise and add to that library in the sky.

Now, go visit Yahoo Answers, Ask.com, and LinkedIn Answers to determine which format and discussions are best for you. Which is easiest for you to use? Which contain the best questions for you to answer? They all have high traffic, so it's up to you.

You can also focus specifically on online Groups and publications that follow your industry. We talked about LinkedIn Groups that are focused on your specialty area. For example, if you are in the fast-growing Energy industry, you might join one of these LinkedIn Groups, which all have discussion areas:

- **Linked:Energy (Energy industry expertise)**
- **Nuclear Power - the next generation**
- **Solar Energy Network**
- **Renewable Energy Network**
- **Energy & Utilities Network**

You should "Google" your industry keywords once a week to determine the most active and relevant topics.

From the Google search results, you'll be able to tell where these topics are being discussed the most: in a LinkedIn Group Discussion? On a conference website? In an online version of a business magazine?

If "smart grid" is in your area of expertise, you might run across this online article from BusinessWeek in one of your keyword searches (See Figure 6-5). Notice that you can "post a comment" on this page, which would be a very "smart" thing to do, given they have an average 12.9 million unique visitors every month.

Bloomberg
Businessweek

SPECIAL REPORT October 5, 2009, 8:18PM EST

The Coming Energy Revolution

Smart-grid technology will bring huge savings to companies as varied as Cisco, PG&E, and Cargill, and to consumers, too. But who will foot the bill?

By Rachael King

View Slide Show ▶

Food producer Cargill is taking a carving knife to its electricity bills. At a plant in Springdale, Ark., where the company handles about 50,000 turkeys a day, electricity bills run more than $2 million a year. But Cargill thinks it can cleave $680,000 from the total by using its own generators on high-demand days.

The secret behind this money-saving plan lies in what's known as the smart grid—a wholesale revamp of the system that distributes energy to homes and businesses around the country. Government bodies and utility providers are in the early stages of this multibillion-dollar upgrade to transform the existing grid into a two-way network where power and information flow in both directions between the utility and the customer, not just from the provider to the user.

SPECIAL REPORT
CEO Guide to Smart Grid Technology

The Coming Energy Revolution

Slide Show: Smart Grid 101

Making Meters Smarter, Home by Home

The Smart Grid Needs Smart Regulations

Podcast: Modernizing the Electricity Grid

STORY TOOLS

💬 post a comment

✉ e-mail this story

🖨 print this story

Figure 6-5

Remember that Google scans large and popular sites (such as this one) all day long. Imagine an employer seeing your comments in BusinessWeek when they search online for experts in smart grid technology .

Are you starting to get the picture about how you can quickly position yourself as an expert candidate to employers?

Blogging

Now that you're blogging on other's blogs (…did you ever think you'd be saying that with a straight face?), you might want to think about starting your own.

Why?

Because…

- It gives people another place to "follow" you and your expertise. Your blog will attract like-minded people and help you build your network.

- It provides a less formal place than a resume or an interview to relay your experiences, knowledge and personality.

- When you are contributing comments in Group discussions, or in another blog, you can refer the readers to your own blog for "more on that subject…"

- Since a blog is actually a website, it provides a platform for you to present documents you may want to share, e.g. your resume, so you'll have a URL address for it.

- The more you write in your blog using your industry keywords, the higher you will appear on search results for those words.

It's fairly easy to start a blog. You can go to one of the "do-it-yourself" sites such as www.weebly.com or www.homestead.com and in a few steps, you will have your own blog.

Then, of course, you have to have something to write about every few days. But don't let this hold you back.

Many people think you have to be an author or a story-teller or a theorist to have a blog. Not so. You just have to have a computer and something to say. Oh, and you need the internet.

In fact, many bloggers just hang out in coffee shops with free internet, and blog about current business or political issues. You like coffee, right?

So, while you are browsing for great blogs where you can post comments, think about starting your own. It will definitely accelerate your visibility if you populate it regularly and talk about topics in your narrow and deep expertise areas.

You're also providing people with another way to *follow you*, which means you're using the internet once again to grow an audience. And your audience becomes part of your network. And as your network expands, you're found in more searches that are done by others within that network.

In other words, what goes around comes around in a very real sense.

So start contributing online.

CHAPTER 7

SEARCH

Do you know where to find the jobs?

Finding jobs

First of all, *you are not looking for a job.* A job is just a paycheck. At your level, you are looking for the next step in your career. You are an executive in transition. You need meaningful work. And, yes, I know... some of you are reading this book to find the magic secret to grabbing a paycheck – any paycheck – as quickly as you can.

Let's talk a bit about desperation.

Desperation is the worst situation to be in. You cannot interview well when you are desperate. You cannot make coherent decisions when you are desperate. And employers and recruiters can smell desperation a mile away.

Try to start working on your *next* career move before you lose/leave your current one. In the recruiting industry, we tend to think that a 2-year tenure is suspiciously short, but that a 5-year stay at a senior level job may mean you're too comfortable and have lost drive and ambition.

So what I'm saying is that there is no excuse for a senior executive to be totally unprepared for a move, whether it's by choice or not – especially in this decade of change. This book is not just for a "point in time" in your career. The concepts are the new normal. In the spirit of responsible counseling, I urge you to think of Chapters 1 through 6 as the base camp for the climb ahead of you.

Career moves will never go back to simply "having a resume updated" for when that recruiter calls.

Keep this book close to your desk for the next few years, and make sure you are constantly updating the base you formed in Chapters 1-4. Work Chapters 5, 6, 8, and 9 into your normal business practices, so that you are connecting, contributing, researching and networking on a regular basis. In fact, THIS chapter becomes the only one you'll get to skip if you do the rest.

You won't need to start a major job search campaign the next time you're downsized or decide to move on (every 3 to 5 years according to the statistics). You'll already be connected to the right people who can move your career forward. You'll have all the latest proof of your expertise online.

Having said all this....If you *are* desperate right now -- for instance, if you have been out of work for several months without doing the things in this book, you have 3 options:

a.   Focus on getting some contract work within your existing network. Skip to Chapter 10 to read more about this.

b.   Hire us immediately. It will be intense. We will perform as many of these 10 Chapters with you as we can in the shortest amount of time.

c.   Go on vacation, get some distance between you and the past, work on inner peace, and come back with the clarity needed to face your future.

Let's continue with the chapter for those who are not likely to lose your grip entirely in the next few weeks for lack of a "job."

So where *do* you find opportunities for your next move?

Of course there are still some job listings in printed newspaper Classified Ads. Most newspapers also have an online version.   But in the past 15 years, that business has been taken over by the online paid-subscription job boards such as Monster and CareerBuilder, and most recently by Craigslist and LinkedIn Jobs.

LinkedIn jobs

By now, you're intimately familiar with LinkedIn and how to build your profile and your network.

Another feature of LinkedIn is their Job Board. You can use the search fields seen on the left of the screen to filter the search results by various job criteria as shown in Figure 7-1 on the next page.

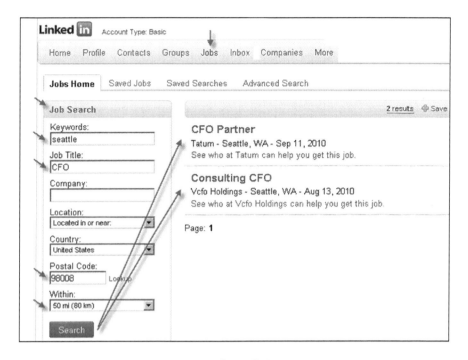

Figure 7-1

In this case, we are looking for a CFO job in the Seattle area.

Indeed and SimplyHired

Indeed.com and SimplyHired.com (and other sites like them) are aggregators that search for and bring together onto one website all jobs from the major job boards (Monster, Careerbuilder, TheLadders, Craigslist, etc.) Hence, the name "aggregators." These sites are usually free for candidates to browse, and are good tools for executives to use.

Here's a tip about Indeed.com and SimplyHired.com.

You can register as a member on these sites (for free) and set up "alerts" to be sent to your email. You define the alerts you want to receive by describing the types of jobs you want to hear about. Be sure to be narrowly focused enough when describing the jobs, as you don't want hundreds of alerts in your inbox every week.

Juju

Juju (www.job-search-engine.com) is a job search engine (not a job posting site) that is becoming more popular. You type in the sort of job you're looking for and it goes out and does the searching real-time for you on employer career sites, and job posting boards, and recruiter websites.

TheLadders

An exclusive site for job seekers who make north of $100K in salary, there is the website called TheLadders.com. Candidates can pay for a subscription and view high end jobs listed there by employers who pay to post.

Executives differ on the value of the subscription, so before signing up, read online reviews on epinions.com, yelp.com, or jibberjobber.com.

Local job listing sites

In addition to the high-traffic global sites such as LinkedIn Jobs and TheLadders.com, and the job posting aggregators mentioned above, there are several smaller regional job pages as well.

Sometimes you may be better served by looking at your local online listings since there will be fewer "eyeballs" on those sites and therefore less competition.

For instance, if you use the Google or Bing or Yahoo search bar, and type in "Seattle Jobs," there are many smaller local job listing sites. Here is a list of some of the sites that are returned from that search request:

http://www.seattle.gov/jobs/ - 21k -
http://www.seattle.gov/parks/jobs/default.htm - 19k -
http://seattlejobs.com/ - 26k -
http://seattle.craigslist.org/ - 30k -
http://www.bizjournals.com/seattle/jobs/ - 82k
http://www.washjob.com/ - 18k -
http://hotjobs.yahoo.com/jobs-l-seattle-WA - 38k -
http://www.seattlejobs.org/ - 7k -
http://www.nwjobs.com/ - 56k -
http://www.Job.com
http://seattle.craigslist.org/ - 30k -
http://washington.careers.org/ - 102k -

Every metropolitan area in the U.S. has websites focusing on local jobs. You can use Google to find local job websites for your city, just as I did. But plowing through tons of jobsites, or even using a jobs aggregator like Indeed.com can be time-consuming and sometimes discouraging.

One of my clients exclaimed to me the other day: "Damn! Looking for a job is a full-time job!" It's true, it can be. Which is why you want to learn as many shortcuts as you can, or even hire someone to set all this up for you..

Let's go back to LinkedIn and Facebook for a minute. They are both free, and easy to use once you are all set up. Yes, you want to post your resume and profiles there to be found, but the next step is to use these sites to actually look for jobs as well.

Groups postings on LinkedIn

Employers have to pay $300 or more to post each of their jobs on the LinkedIn Job Board. This is the "Jobs" tab at the top of your LinkedIn page. What internal company recruiters have discovered is that they can post and discuss their open jobs *for free* in the LinkedIn **Groups** and **subgroups**.

So yes, you can follow the main LinkedIn Jobs page along with millions of other hopefuls. However, if you have more than 10 years of experience, you probably fit into several of the business Groups on LinkedIn, so go to the Groups that you have joined, and look in their job listings (e.g. Figure 7-2).

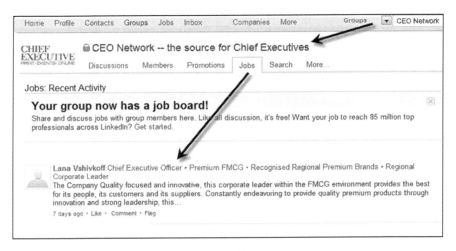

Figure 7-2

If you clicked on the link at the end of the arrow in Figure 7-2 , you would see that a real person named Lana is announcing a CEO opening:

CEO job opening discussed within a LinkedIn Group

Chief Executive Officer • Premium FMCG • Recognised Regional Premium Brands • Regional Corporate Leader

The Company
Quality focused and innovative, this corporate leader within the FMCG environment provides the best for its people, its customers and its suppliers. Constantly endeavoring to provide quality premium products through innovation and strong leadership, this organization has been a market leader for the just under 30 years providing unique brands. Its mission is to increase vertically and introduce new exciting categories to its product line over the next decade.

The Opportunity
As the Chief Executive Officer, you will be an astute business individual capable of driving a successful FMCG business within a competitive business arena operating within the GCC, MENA and Levant regions. Your ability to thrive in the face of business challenges and adversity will be highly regarded as will your ability to develop and filter strategy and vision throughout the organization for the next decade.

Ideally, you will be results driven with the ability to work within a culturally diverse workforce and hold over 10 years experience within a senior management position within the FMCG environment. Additionally you will also hold an MBA. You will also be a charismatic leader who has the ability to make key decisions at the right time based on qualified business and market information.

Please note only shortlisted candidates will be contacted.

Please send expressions of interest to lanaXX@company.com or contact Lana directly on +971 X XXX 8860.

Figure 7-3

Notice that the poster gives out her direct email address and phone number at the bottom of the posting! Ta-dahhh! A real human to contact instead of submitting your resume to a robot screening system.

And here we have another reason for you to join relevant Groups and their subgroups on LinkedIn – so that you can hear about these jobs immediately, and deal directly with the recruiters or hiring managers who are posting the jobs or discussing them online in LinkedIn.

ExecuNet

ExecuNet is another executive-focused website, also with a LinkedIn Jobs page that puts job seekers in direct touch with company recruiters and/or hiring managers.

See Figure 7-4 and/or go to their LinkedIn page by typing in "Executive Suite" in the Groups search field.

Jobs: Recent Activity
Your group now has a job board!

Share and discuss jobs with group members here. Like all discussion, it's free! Want your job to reach 85 million top professionals across LinkedIn?

 Drew GENERAL MANAGER – TEXAS $100K+ LUXURY HOSPITALITY Any recommendations would be welcomed. LOOKING FOR SOMEONE WITH LUXURY GM OR F&B EXPERIENCE TO OVERSEE MULTIPLE HOSPITALITY PROPERTIES. MUST SPEAK SPANISH AND ENGLISH....

 Micah General Manager – Brazil – San Paolo
Dynamic and growing client in Latin America is seeking a General Manager to oversee their entire country's sales and marketing efforts. Experience growing sales through distributors and having dealt with gaining Regulatory approval is an absolute must. Aggressive,...

Figure 7-4

As you can see, the LinkedIn website is very valuable to you as a job seeker if you know how to use it to find job listings at your level and in your area of interest.

Remember: Join the online LinkedIn Groups in your geographic and talent areas. Look at the "Jobs" tabs within those Groups. Respond to the posters directly.

Facebook

There is much debate about whether Facebook is just a social site for the younger generation or whether it is a valuable tool for the serious business person, and even for corporations.

When you find things like this highlighted on Facebook, you start to realize it's not just for kids anymore:

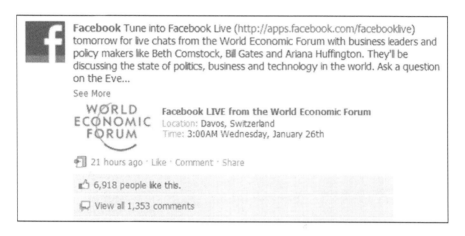

Figure 7-5

As you can see in Figure 7-5, nearly 7000 people read it and appreciated the message and over 1300 people commented on this post. And no, they are not all college kids.

In fact, there are many corporations (See Cisco below) who use Facebook to attract "followers." A new organizational department is cropping up in many companies with names like Digital Marketing, E-Marketing, Social Marketing and new titles within those such as "Community Manager."

Here's an example:

Welcome to Cisco's Official Facebook Page!
I'm Lindsay K. the community manager for the page!

Visit us also on the following sites:
http://newsroom.cisco.com/
http://socialmedia.cisco.com/
http://blogs.cisco.com/
http://twitter.com/ciscosystems

Cisco uses Facebook (Figure 7-6) to build an online community of followers (already numbering more than 130,000 people), to which they can push out news items, announcements, and yes, even job openings.

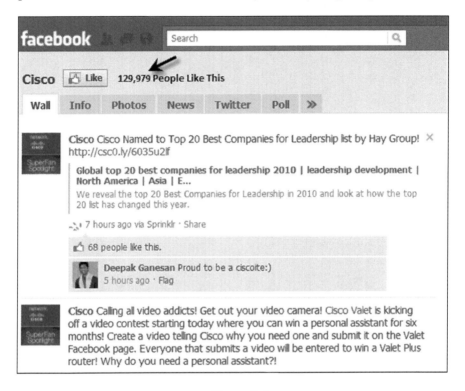

Figure 7-6

So, you'll want to go to Facebook and join the online communities of those employers who interest you. Remember this discussion when reading the next chapter on researching interesting employers.

BranchOut

Recently Facebook has added a networking tool called BranchOut (Figure 7-7), which is similar to the Connections feature of LinkedIn, in that it leverages the power of your Facebook network to reveal potential professional contacts.

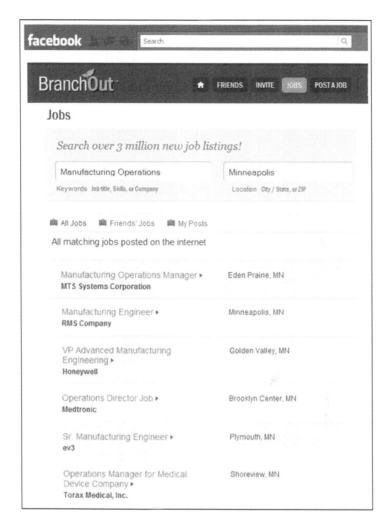

Figure 7-7

The BranchOut (Facebook) approach to job listing is to piggy-back on one of the jobs aggregators that we talked about: Indeed.com. When you search for a job through BranchOut, you really are using the power of Indeed.com to search all jobs found on the internet, which is convenient.

The Facebook/BranchOut logic is this: Since there are more than 600 million Facebook members, odds are good that someone in that company where the perfect job exists will be a Facebook member. Therefore you can connect with that employee through Facebook and gain a "connection" to the hiring manager or recruiter.

Not unlike the LinkedIn theory.

Twitter

Twitter is a relatively new communication tool that allows a user to send and receive short (140-character) messages on a computer or mobile device. The business world has adopted it as a quick way to make real-time announcements to their interested communities.

For instance, several internal recruiting departments now "tweet" out a message as soon as a job opens up. All the followers of that company will immediately receive the short message about the job and can click a link within the message to find out more if they wish.

How to become a follower?

You, as a job seeker, can go to www.Twitter.com and sign up for free. Then you can "follow" employers who are of interest to you and receive their tweets. Their tweets are simply short messages about what's happening inside the company today – a new product release, or a presentation they're doing at a conference today, or a new job that was posted today.

Twitter is growing rapidly. Employers are including Twitter into their hiring strategies just as they are LinkedIn and Facebook. They are building their online communities with these tools.

Yes, their fan clubs then become captive audiences for their marketing pitches, but their community also becomes the first to hear about job openings through their Twitter accounts.

So, if you are a Twitter follower of that company, you will receive these short messages in your Twitter account online or on your mobile device *as soon as they are posted.*

You can also do job searches in Twitter the same way you do with job search engines -- by entering keywords in the Search field as shown in Figure 7-8 on the next page.

In this case I am a job seeker looking for a financial management job somewhere near Seattle, WA. When I hit the Search button, Twitter returns a list of "tweets" – 140-character messages – that have been sent out by companies regarding their open jobs.

Since the Twitter messages are so short, you just click on the links in the message to take you to the actual job posting on that company's career website.

You can liken a job tweet to the *alert* an airline sends to your cell phone when the departure time has changed. The difference is that job tweets are always *good* news.

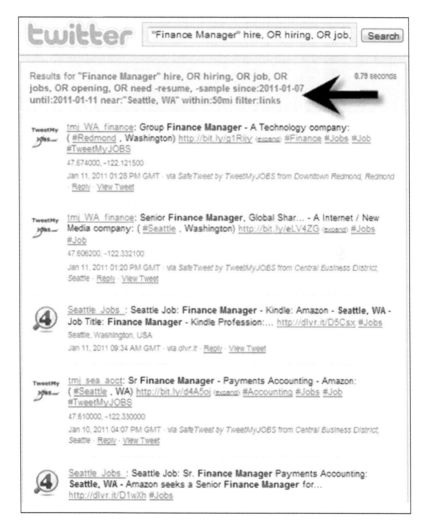

Figure 7-8

In addition, you want to get "followed" by hiring managers and internal recruiters. How do you get them to follow you?

Three ways:

1. If you notice on your LinkedIn profile, you can display your Twitter name as well. When you do the connecting work of chapter 5, and when you do the research work of Chapter 8, you are adding people to your network. Many of these new connections will click on that Twitter name in your profile and follow your tweets.
2. Contribute. If you have a Twitter account, you will be tweeting (sending out a link to) every article that you post anywhere else on the web, and any post that you add to your blog or others' (as you learned in chapter 6). Some of these will be re-tweeted. It's the same six-degrees theory that we discussed in Chapter 4. If you send messages (tweets) to your followers on Twitter, they may also "re-tweet" your message to other appropriate people in their own follower lists. And the people who like your tweets will become followers.
3. Follow *them*. Call it ego or courtesy, but when you follow another person, they generally will check you out online to see if you are also worth following. If you have a large network, they will generally return the follow. Or if your recent tweets are professional and meaningful in your area of expertise, they will follow you.

If all this sounds complicated, you can register for free on a site such as www.TweetAJob.com or www.TweetMyJOBS.com. These services will ask you what city you'd like to work in, and what type of job you're looking for. Then they do all the search work for you. Any time an announcement is made on Twitter about that type of job in your location you'll receive an immediate message – a tweet – with a link to the job.

LinkUp

LinkUp is not LinkedIn.

It is a new job search engine that purportedly pulls jobs directly from more than 20,000 employer websites. Their promise is that all their job postings are from real companies, and are guaranteed not to be scams, or work-from-home offers, or from staffing agencies.

Now that we've discussed a few of these in detail, you have a resource list to start using in finding those perfect job openings.

And what do you do when you find an open position that's of interest to you?

- Look at the keywords in the job description and make sure they are also on your resume and LinkedIn profile (if it's truthful). Remember that although you want to be chosen for your total asset value, you still have to get through the first parts of today's selection system.
- Go back to your network to see who you are connected with in that company.
- Do some further research on the employer! (Coming up in the next chapter.)

CHAPTER 8

RESEARCH

How do you research a potential employer?

OK, now that you know what your true asset value is to an employer, it's time to turn your focus to researching companies that match you.

Why? Because in this day and age it's really up to you to go out and find the opportunities… and to present yourself to the world.

Used to be that you could call the few niche recruiters in your industry and count on them to know who was hiring.

Then you would have a brief phone conversation with them, they would write up some notes about you and fax your resume over to employers who would pay a fee for the introduction.

Well, employers are looking for you on the internet now, cutting out the middleman and the fee.

AND they are posting their jobs on the internet, so you can be up to speed on who's hiring just as quickly as most recruiters.

So unless you think you're worth an extra $50,000 (headhunter fee) to the employer over your competition, you might want to keep reading.

There are 2 ways to go about researching employers:

1.   Find employers you are interested in, and do enough research on them "to have an intelligent conversation with their CEO."

2.   Find job openings in your specialty area, as we saw in Chapter 7, and then research *those particular employers.*

Either way works and, in fact, both strategies can be exercised at the same time. You can spend some time scanning the job openings, which we discussed in the last chapter, and also focus some of your attention on the types of employers you'd like to target.

1. Researching employers you might like to work for

What do *you* need to know about an employer in order to determine whether you'd be interested in working there?

- Size?
- Location?
- Mission?
- Product or service (does it match your expertise area?)
- Financial health (would you get a consistent paycheck?)
- Management style (Remember the exercise for Figure 2-3?)

There are many lists you can find, especially through your city's library system, that will categorize companies in your area by industry type and/or product type and size.

And there are hundreds of lists online. A favorite Google search of mine is: "best companies to work for in [your city]."

For more newsy data, you can also go on the internet and look up phrases from your industry (e.g. "financial services") plus a few other keywords like "record earnings" and "growth" and "expansion."

Here's one: (Q4 earnings soar 2011 report "financial services"). Go to your computer and type that into your Google browser. Since it is Q1 2011 at the time of this writing, you will see a list of news reports about financial services companies who had a good Q4 in 2010. If I were to launch that search, the results would feature Seattle area companies because Google knows where I'm sitting right now.

In addition, you can choose your favorite source, as in Forbes or Wall Street Journal or Associated Press like this: (Q4 "profits up" forestry *site:reuters.com*)

And you're off and running on your research.

Zoominfo

You can take a more direct approach with tools like Zoominfo (www.zoominfo.com).

Type in your location and industry keywords to find companies in your geographic location and industry sector.

In Figure 8-1 (next page) for example, we found 98 companies in Seattle that are in the technology manufacturing industry.

ZoomInfo search

Figure 8-1

You can browse companies here and choose which to research further based on the company summary, revenue, and employee size that suits you best.

One of the nice things about Zoominfo is that once you focus on a company, you can click the "Find People" tab and retrieve a list of their employees and contact info. (And what do you do with those names...? Right! Find them online in their blogs and Groups and "follow" them, and/or invite them into your LinkedIn network.)

Hoovers

One of the standard research tools for company data is Hoovers at www.hoovers.com. A free trial will get you location, contact, management, competitors, history, overview and some financial data about your target company. And you can pay for a subscription to get more details including direct contact information for the management team.

In Figure 8-2, we've targeted Applied Discovery, Inc. using Hoovers.

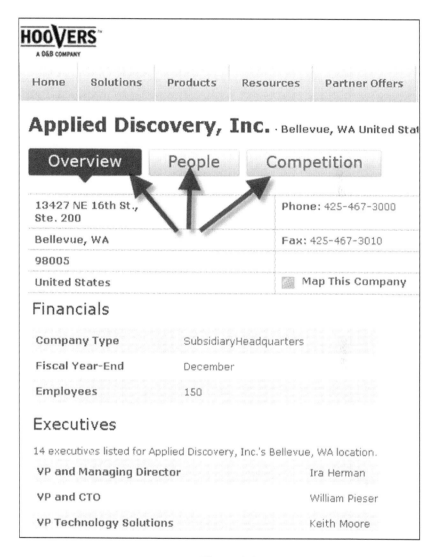

Figure 8-2

Once you know the executives' names, and a bit about the company, you can choose to look them up on LinkedIn and invite them to your network to start a relationship.

No, it's not rude. It's not an intrusion if you do this in a respectful manner. We'll talk more about that in the next chapter about Networking.

Business Journals

The official Business Journal spans 41 metropolitan areas and is a good site to visit in doing company research for questions about companies' general health, innovation, and problems.

One of the tabs on their site is the "Local Directory" tab. So we clicked on Seattle to look up Applied Discovery, Inc. again.

Here we find news articles about them over a 3-year span, which adds another dimension to our knowledge of their history. These articles tell stories about their competitors, their clients and their employees, giving us some extra insight about their corporate culture and history.

Figure 8-3

2. Researching employers who have job openings

Let's say you've found a job that looks interesting, so now you want to research that employer:

- Who is funding them?
- Who is on their Board?
- Are they public or private?
- Local, national, or global?
- Who runs the joint?
- How big is the company?
- What is the background of the management team? What companies did they come from?
- Who are their competitors?
- What is their mission statement?
- How well are they doing? What is their stage of maturity?
- How innovative are their products and services?
- What are the current hurdles they are facing?

Website

Of course, if you already know the name of the company, the most direct route to concentrated information is the company's own website.

Focus on their mission statement, their most recent press releases, and the backgrounds of their management team. This will tell you pretty quickly whether or not you are interested.   But chances are their website would leave out any negative press or product problems or news of unrest in the ranks.

So you'll want to get third party perspectives and some "soft" information in addition to the hard facts.

YouTube

A good source for that is YouTube, believe it or not. Just go to www.youtube.com and type in the company name in the browser field as in Figure 8-4.

Often you'll find taped interviews with a board member, or an employee or client, such as this YouTube video regarding a company called Applied Discovery.

Figure 8-4

And then there are the "insider info" sites like glassdoor (www.glassdoor.com) where employees speak frankly about their companies and rank their CEOs. Of course, we take these sites with a grain of salt, but there is something to be said for statistical volume.

See what I mean in Figure 8-5 on the next page.

Figure 8-5

In Figure 8-5 we see that 83% of 1,544 Deloitte reviewers (employees) think their CEO is doing a good job, whereas only 39% of 181 Safeway reviewers are happy with the work of their CEO. Do with this information whatever you like, but these types of data points are all pieces of the puzzle in figuring out the fit – the corporate culture match, the attitude, the mission, the health – of that company and your next move.

Direct contact info

It's nice to know the names of the CEOs and hiring managers, but the next step is getting their direct contact information.

So how would you go about finding contact information for the hiring managers or recruiters inside the company you're targeting?

1. LinkedIn
   a. Use the "Company" search function. Type in the name of the company to retrieve a list of all employees of that company.
   b. Check your network to see who knows those people and can connect you to them.
   c. Once you are "connected" to them as a 1st degree contact, your view of their profile page will display their email address.
2. Hoovers
   a. We discussed this a few pages ago, but it's good to remember that Hoovers can provide you with lists of people and their contact information
3. Zoominfo
   a. Likewise with Zoominfo. You can search on company name and retrieve contact information for people in that organization.

You can buy lists that provide this information.

- Industry Specific Directories. There are hundreds of company lists on the web for every industry. Here are a few examples:

  IndustryWeek.com (Manufacturing)
  MediaPost.com (Media)

- Location Specific Directories. Every state and city has business directories that you can find through the BBB or chambers of commerce. Among the best to use for choosing employers are the Business Journal sites around the country at www.bizjournals.com. It's a little more work than choosing from a list, but browsing through articles about local companies gives you data and names that may not otherwise be found.

There are many services that collect and verify lists of *corporate executives* for use in building lead lists for sales, or target lists for recruiters. Why not use them for your job search purposes?

For instance, for a dollar per name, Sheila Greco sells lists of executives, categorized by industry and company. You can view and purchase the lists here: http://www.sgaexecutivetracker.com/A-Z.jsp?INDEXLETTER=N

Google

Search engines also allow us to perform "educated guessing" about email addresses. If you find a company you'd like to work for -- e.g. RealNetworks – go to the Google search bar and type in:

"*@realnetworks.com 206" as in Figure 8-6

The " * " acts as a wildcard for picking up anyone's name at RealNetworks, and the "206" narrows the results to those in Seattle, where RealNetworks is located.

Figure 8-6

This simple search returns several RealNetworks employees and their email addresses *and* phone numbers. This helps us to determine the internal naming conventions that RealNetworks uses for its internal email system, which in this case, seems to be "first initial + last name @ real.com" or "first initial + last name @ realnetworks.com" as in bhankes@real.com and mcharlier@real.com and epheasant@real.com.

So, now you can go to LinkedIn, and find the apparent hiring manager or recruiter for the jobs at RealNetworks that you might be interested in..

For example, let's say you're interested in a Director of Merchandising position and the job description says that it would report to the VP of Marketing.

1. Go to the Advanced People Search page on LinkedIn.
   a) Type "VP Marketing" for title
   b) Type "RealNetworks" for company
   c) Type "98121" as zipcode (from Figure 8-6)

2. LinkedIn will bring up the name of the VP Marketing of RealNetworks: Jane Doe.

3. Now you have a pretty good idea that her direct email address is JDoe@realnetworks.com.

But wait! I'm not suggesting that you rush off and email all the VPs around town!

Hold your horses.

We'll talk about what we do with all this contact information in Chapters 9 and 10.

CHAPTER 9

NETWORK

How do you plan to get networked to targeted opportunities?

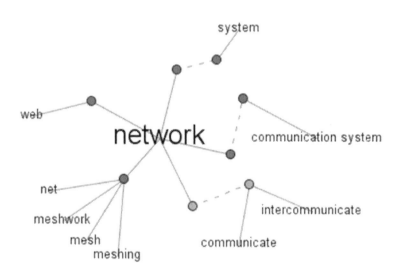

Yes, the concept of "networking" is all the rage now, but what does it really mean and how do you go about it?

Guess what? You're already doing it!

The outcome of everything you've started to do (or continued to do) in Chapters 1-8 is that you are now becoming more visible. You are networking your way into the limelight.

As in Figure 9-1, you're connecting with people, following them on their websites and LinkedIn Discussions and Twitter. You're blogging and commenting and contributing your advice in your Groups and on Wikis and even in trade magazines.

And the more you do this, the sooner you'll be visible to those who need you.

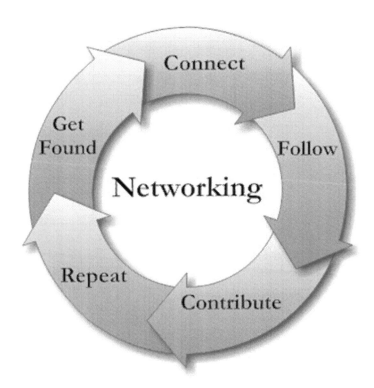

Figure 9-1

But how do you get the ball rolling? You've learned the strategy, and some of the tactics, but how do you start putting it all into action?

Physical networking

Let's talk a bit about physical (traditional) networking for a minute. It's important. And it's the easiest way to start, since you're probably already doing these things to some extent:

- Having coffee meetings with business contacts and friends;
- Joining public projects in your community;
- Serving on boards of schools, local businesses, or non-profits;
- Attending industry conferences and seminars; and
- Being active in your faith community.

This is your physical network.

Since, as we established earlier, "looking for a job" can be a full time job in itself, you will have to determine where you'll get the most benefit in your physical network. For instance, you may benefit mentally from the camaraderie factor while attending get-togethers with other unemployed executives, but that's probably not the quickest way to move *financially* forward.

Many of our clients actually schedule their days as if they were still in a 9-5 job, planning each day's coffee meetings, online research, and phone calls. Mapping the physical network onto a calendar can help keep the momentum going by providing target dates for completing important portfolio pieces. This is very helpful, in that it provides some structure (sanity) in a stressful time.

It also helps "keep you out of the quicksand" – the phase when you feel you are being sucked down further in spite of your strenuous efforts to get out of the hole. Not a fun stage, but very common in the executive job seeker's life today.

Go back and look at your physical network and make sure you've invited the appropriate people from that network into your online LinkedIn and/or BranchOut networks.

Online Networking

Online networking is the combination of all the things we've discussed in the previous chapters:

- Inviting people into your LinkedIn and BranchOut networks;
- Joining online Groups;
- Participating in online discussions in LinkedIn, and your industry chat forums, and in trade magazines;
- "Following" targeted influencers and companies;
- Blogging;
- Connecting with networked recruiters;
- Contributing answers on the question sites such as Answers.com;
- Discussing new job postings found in your Groups and subgroups and industry forums; and
- Linking to employees within companies of interest.

The combination of physical and online networking is the key to success.

In the next few pages, I'm going to give you a guide that may help in setting up your networking schedule.

Your networking universe is in this simple spreadsheet in Figure 9-2. I have divided it into 3 categories of contacts:

    a. Those who are *existing contacts* of yours, socially and in your business sphere;

    b. New contacts that you are meeting through *physical networking;* and

    c. New contacts that you are finding through your *online research:* friends of friends, internal recruiters, and hiring managers you've uncovered in your searches.

You should make a similar spreadsheet and fill in one name in a blank space every day. This will give you some structure and a way to keep track on a daily basis of what you've accomplished.

Keep in mind that this exercise is not just for this particular job search. It sets up your ongoing networking activity shown above in Figure 9-1 as the basis for your future career moves.

Existing Physical Network	Monday	Tuesday
Alum contacts	Jane Doe	Joe Smith
Sports contacts	Kerry Fee	Harlan D.
Hobby contacts		
Church contacts		
Social contacts		
General Business contacts		
Your industry contacts		
New Physical Network Contacts		
Conference attendees		
Social event attendees		
Trade show attendees		
New business introductions		
New Online Network Contacts from Research and Introductions		
2nd and 3rd degree network		
Internal recruiters		
Companies		
Hiring managers		
Industry influencers		

Figure 9-2

In the third category, the new online network contacts, we are talking about people and companies you don't yet know. You will find these through the work you have done in the previous chapters.

Now, let's talk about *when* you do *what* with *whom*.

Networking does *not* mean sending out your resume to all the contacts you've made. Please don't. You will just get buried in the system with everyone else.

Your networking approach will differ slightly within each category of your connections. Examine Figure 9-3 (next page) for a minute, and I'll explain.

141

Your Networking Timeline	Send a nice email or LinkedIn message	invite into your LinkedIn and BranchOut networks	Have coffee	"follow" on their website, on Twitter, and in Discussions	Contribute by responding on their blogs, articles, and comments	Quote them, repost them, refer to them on your own blog	Send them your complete profile or showcase	Ask them for assistance in connecting
Existing contacts								
Alum contacts	Do 2nd	Do 1st					Do 4th	Do 3rd
Sports contacts	Do 2nd	Do 1st					Do 4th	Do 3rd
Hobby contacts	Do 2nd	Do 1st					Do 4th	Do 3rd
Church contacts	Do 1st	Do 3rd	Do 2nd				Do 4th	Do 3rd
Social contacts	Do 1st	Do 3rd	Do 2nd					Do 4th
All Business contacts		Do 1st						
Your industry contacts	Do 3rd	Do 1st		Do 2nd	Do 4th			Do 5th
New Contacts								
Conference attendees	Do 1st	Do 3rd		Do 2nd	Do 4th			Do 5th
Social event attendees	Do 1st	Do 4th	Do 2nd	Do 3rd				Do 5th
Trade show attendees	Do 1st	Do 3rd		Do 2nd	Do 4th			Do 5th
New business introductions	Do 1st	Do 4th	Do 3rd	Do 2nd				Do 5th
Researched contacts								
2nd and 3rd degree network	Do 1st	Do 2nd		Do 4th	Do 3rd			Do 5th
Internal recruiters		Do 1st		Do 3rd	Do 2nd		Do 4th	
Companies				Do 1st	Do 2nd	Do 3rd		
Hiring managers		Do 3rd		Do 2nd	Do 1st	Do 4th	Do 5th	
Industry influencers		Do 4th		Do 1st	Do 2nd	Do 3rd	Do 6th	Do 5th

Figure 9-3

In Figure 9-3 I'm giving you a set of guidelines to follow in your networking. These aren't set in stone and the order can be moved a bit, *but…*

…notice that you don't even begin to ask for assistance from your connections until you've done some give-and-take with them. You need to earn their aid, especially with your new contacts. Even with your existing contacts, you need to set the stage with an explanatory email and an inviting reason to connect before asking them for assistance in your career move.

All the tips for Connecting and Contributing in chapters 5 and 6 are very important steps and *must precede* the pitching of your profile to your contacts.

In the best of all worlds, you'd never have to ask for anyone's help. You'd be so connected that you would just put out the word that you may be available, and your phone would start ringing.

Like in the old days.

From Bedlam to Boardroom

CHAPTER 10

PITCH

Now push yourself into play.

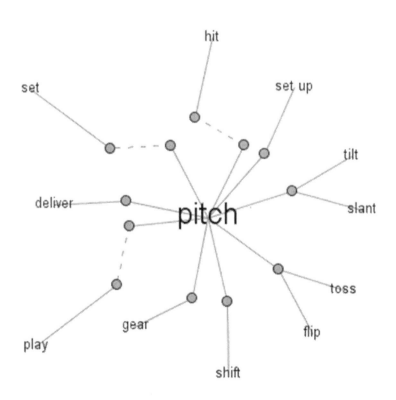

Look how far you've come!

- We've guided you through the painful part of dismantling and reconstructing your persona.
- You have a killer resume and online profile
- You've positioned these documents strategically so they will be found.
- If we've built an InterviewStudio showcase for you, you have an elegant and data-rich profile to send out as your executive brand.
- You are quickly building your authority status online.
- You've put yourself on alert so that job postings will come to your inbox.
- You have a growing network of business contacts and internal recruiters.
- You are actively following a number of potential employers closely.

Yes, you've done a lot of work, but the real success is measured in the number of interviews you obtain -- and how quickly you obtain them -- from doing the work in this book.

If you are a current client, this is the point where the Executive Program injects you aggressively into the job market. And we/you really need the groundwork of the previous chapters in order to do this.

If you're doing this on your own, keep the guide in Figure 9-3 in mind. When you're ready to start the "pitch" phase of sending your profile and asking for assistance, here's what you do.

Park your profile

You need to be able to point people to *one place* where they will find your resume and other documents you want them to see. Your LinkedIn profile is not enough. It serves the purpose of getting you connected to business resources. But if you're seriously looking for a job, a new career, or an avenue to income, you'll want to point your LinkedIn visitors to a page that is all about your quest, with backup documentation.

InterviewStudio can be used for such a purpose. Go back to chapter 4 and look at the optional assets you can store there for a one-stop look at all your asset value. InterviewStudio has a unique URL address. And it is a simple link that you can email to people and put on your LinkedIn profile page.

If you've ventured into the blogosphere and built your own blog site, then you can park all your documents there. The point is to have a single URL address that will lead to your complete package with one click.

OR, if you don't have an InterviewStudio showcase or a blog/web page, no problem. Go to a site where you can easily build a web page or blog for free, like Weebly (www.weebly.com). You can choose one of their templates and be ready to publish *within an hour*. Seriously. In a very short time, you can create a workable landing page to bring together all these things:

- A full cover letter and explanation of what you are looking for and why;
- Your full resume;
- Letters of recommendation;
- Portfolio documents;
- Business Plans;
- Links to YouTube videos you've created in order to deliver a message;
- Links to an online profile such as InterviewStudio; and
- The results of any recent skills or personality tests.

For example, Valerie Smith may have a LinkedIn profile, but she also wants her own landing page that she can control and make private.

Using s self-building site such as the one mentioned above, she took a few hours, chose a design and just began loading documents and content that she wants to share with hiring managers – and not necessarily with the 100 million folks on LinkedIn.

You can see in Figure 10-1 that she now has a landing page, and she can send the URL link to people she chooses.

She also chose categories she wants listed in the black bar across the top of the page. The screen shot in Figure 10-1 is her content for the "Objective" tab. The next screen shot (Figure 10-2) shows the documents that she chose to include for viewing by those she invites.

Figure 10-1

Valerie can park documents, certifications, videos, and charts here:

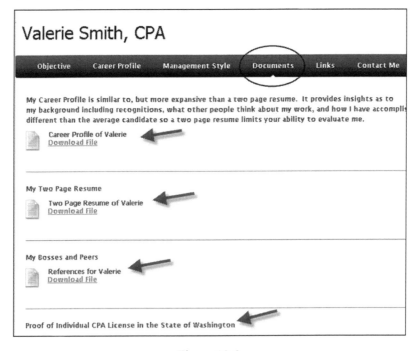

Figure 10-2

Tweet yourself out to your Twitter network

When you "tweet" a message out to the Twitter audience (now numbering over 175 million) you use 140 characters to get a message across:

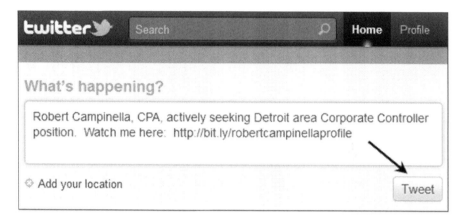

Figure 10-3

You simply type a message and click the Tweet button. You can either add your location using the feature on the lower left corner of Figure 10-3 or you can mention it in the body of your tweet as Robert Campinella did.

How do you get your message to 175 million tweeters? Well, at your level, you probably don't want to. You want to tweet this type of message to a smaller targeted audience.

In fact, you may want to turn on the privacy feature in your Twitter account as in Figure 10-4:

Tweet Privacy	☐ Protect my tweets
	Only let people whom i approve follow my tweets. If this is checked, your future tweets will not be available publicly. Tweets posted previously may still be publicly visible in some places.
	Save

Figure 10-4

Then you can choose which of your followers to send a private message to. You can only send a private message to those who follow you, which is why it's important for you to encourage hiring managers and internal recruiters and industry influencers to follow you.

Announce your status on LinkedIn

Much like we saw with Twitter, you can send a message out to your LinkedIn network – all of them or selected members -- once you have your LinkedIn profile populated with the necessary ingredients:

- Your detailed chronological job history;
- Your photo;
- Your heading;
- Your specialty area keywords;
- Your growing list of connections;
- Your recommendations;
- Your member Groups; and
- Your uploaded documents.

Now you are ready to pitch yourself out to certain connections, as in Figure 10-5.

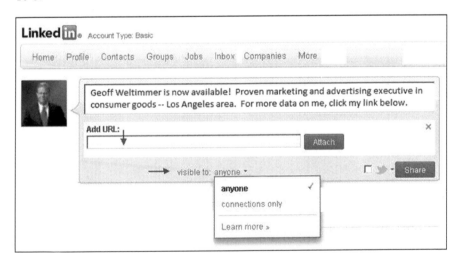

Figure 10-5

In the "Add URL" field in Figure 10-5, Geoff can now place the link to that website or blog where he "parked his profile" using the information earlier in this chapter.

Mention your status in appropriate blogs and Groups

Since we just discussed LinkedIn, don't forget about the Groups and subgroups you have been active in. Usually they have a Jobs tab of their own, and discussions around those job openings.

Script a message like the one above and send it out to members of those Groups and/or mention your status and web link within discussion posts.

You have also joined and participated in industry blogs by now (Chapter 6), so you have earned the right to do a bit of self-promotion. Choose those industry blogs with the most members living in your geographic area.

Do the same thing as above. Send out a BTW (By the way...) message to those members of influence, and let them know that it's OK to send your information on.

Send out a high impact email campaign

We've all received them – those nice looking graphic newsletters that pop up in our email. If you can design a simple impactful message that doesn't take all day to render properly on the page, you can get some real mileage this way.

Send out a high impact email, something like Figure 10-6. (You can export all your LinkedIn connections' email addresses into your email program or just use your Outlook or other email program contacts).

I suggest including your photo in an email like this for two reasons:
a) It personalizes your email a bit so viewers are less likely to hit the delete button, especially if they have their email in preview mode and can see the nice layout before actually opening the message.
b) If you have a common name, and/or there are others on LinkedIn with your name, this photo will help them recognize your profile when searching for more information. Point: be sure to use the same LinkedIn photo in your high impact email.

Notice that all of Valerie's information is just a click away for the viewer.

Templates like these can be found online by Googling "high impact email templates." One source of templates is templatezone.com.

Figure 10-6

YouTube yourself

As of February 2011, YouTube was counting 490 million unique users worldwide *per month*, who were racking up an estimated 92 billion page views each month[15].

These are astounding numbers, and you may dismiss them as "kids just having fun," but video is not just for entertainment. In a sound-bite society, the news sources now compete online to provide up-to-the-minute news to a global audience of billions.

---

[15] Statistics from Mashable: http://mashable.com/2011/02/19/youtube-facts/

Not only the traditional television networks, but sites like Bloomberg's (http://www.bloomberg.com/video/) and Wall Street Journal (http://online.wsj.com/video-center) and Forbes (http://video.forbes.com/recentVideo) are competing for viewers and the accompanying online advertising dollars.

Social media marketing with video on YouTube and Facebook is a growing e-marketing strategy for many corporations. With hundreds of millions of viewers who will watch for at least a few seconds, it's logical for employers to build online communities and feed them short, informational video content – about their products, or their weekly specials, or even about their job openings.

Why not use the same strategy on those employers?

Have someone help you capture on video a discussion of your Narrow and Deep skill sets. Tell stories about the business problems you've tackled and solved. Then upload the video clip to YouTube and send the link (URL address) to your selected audience of LinkedIn, BranchOut, and Twitter contacts. Figure 10-7 shows an example.

Figure 10-7

This executive used the InterviewStudio platform to develop a video, but you could have any professional videographer help you. Video clips should be no longer than 3 minutes, and preferably only 2. Most viewers will watch the first 10 seconds to see if it's worth the time, so you'll need to pack some punch at the front end.

Are you worried about age discrimination?

Tools like YouTube and Twitter may seem age-inappropriate to you for an executive job search. They're not. Obama uses them to market his messages, and look at all the gray hair he has!

And now we've arrived at the subject of age discrimination, or "ageism" which I promised you back in Chapter 6 that I would address here.

Age is both an asset and a liability.

I have rented a home to four people in their twenties. They are full of life and hope and self-confidence and newly acquired educational knowledge. I would not hire any of them.

Why? Because my practice is all about executive level business people, and not one of these young people would be able to relate to your experience, your accomplishments, your career goals, your setbacks, or the pressure you're under right now.

So, yes. I discriminate against them because I think they couldn't do the job. They could learn the scripts, but they could not empathize -- they could not really relate to you.

Energy, influence, and atrophy

On the executive level, there is discrimination as well. But is it "age" that is the problem?

I like to describe the issue as one of "energy, influence and atrophy" rather than age.

People like to hire others who are just like them.

If you don't match the high energy, excitement, and passion of the rest of the company, the hiring managers perceive you as having no energy, no excitement, and no passion. Most likely, this is not the case. Most likely, you have learned over the years to think before you speak, consider alternatives before making quick decisions, do some research on solutions, and always consider the downsides of each. You call this prudence. They may call it slow. Strike one.

If you have let yourself go physically, many hiring managers may feel that your mental agility has atrophied as well. Seriously. It's not age discrimination. It's their perception of your overall energy and stamina, especially in a highly taxing position and/or one with a lot of travel and activity. Strike two.

If you don't use the language, the acronyms, the newest industry buzzwords, they may think you are outdated. Or that you have lost the drive to keep up with new things. I knew an executive who was one of the first brilliant architects of the client-server age. He went for an interview with a large software vendor, but he didn't describe his work in the newest language of distributed technology – "cloud computing." Strike three.

Companies like to hire people who bring a batch of business along with them. Or people who are well-known and have a large amount of influence. If you haven't written a book or published papers or obtained patents or been on TV for your expertise, it is imperative that you have a huge following online. Chapter 6. Enough said.

And then there are the effects of the current economic instability.

If you have more experiences than hiring managers in your area of expertise, it can be intimidating. They may think:

> What if he questions me on my decisions?
> What if he won't do what I ask him to do?
> What if he doesn't respect me as his manager?
> What if he calls me on my bull during a meeting?
> OR
> What if the board replaces me with him on the next layoff?

So be careful when you start to think age discrimination is taking place.

That will just make things worse. You'll be defensive during your interviews without realizing it. And what *you* might perceive as "age discrimination" might be a hiring manager's response to what you project in the areas of energy, influence, and atrophy.

Stay current on your industry's products and services. Read blogs and follow companies online. Don't give up.

The suggestions in this book *do* work.

One of our clients, a senior financial manager candidate, recently sent us her updated statistics from LinkedIn. We had begun working with her in December 2010. Her LinkedIn profile and resume were "OK" but she wasn't getting the notice that she wanted.

During the next few weeks, she diligently followed everything we told you in Chapters 1 – 4.

Within sixty days, her LinkedIn visitor statistics showed dramatic improvement:

Linkedin Stats		
Week Ending	**Search Appearances**	**Notes**
10/17/2010	36	Prior to Colleen's Advice
10/24/2010	92	" " " "
10/31/2010	88	" " " "
11/7/2010	139	" " " "
11/14/2010	99	" " " "
11/21/2010	36	" " " "
11/28/2010	151	Profile Update Activity, Contacts clicking to see me
12/5/2010	141	" " " "
12/12/2010	93	" " " "
12/19/2010	218	After 6 Endorsements, no specific key words
12/26/2010	31	Christmas Week
1/2/2011	**236**	After 9 endorsements, no specific key words
1/9/2011	**273**	Key words added and Google profile links to box.net
1/16/2011	**234**	After 10 endorsements and addition of better groups
1/23/2011	**432**	More job search activity among HR professionals
1/30/2011	**485**	Wow ←

She is appearing in more than 400 searches every week – that's 60 times a day that her profile comes up in someone's search results... which is why her phone is starting to ring.

And here is what she wrote to us after a week of phone calls from interested employers:

"...My online profile "search to visit ratio" has sky-rocketed ... I am no longer anonymous and am enjoying a new prominent position in the search engines, at the level that I want to be found... Never having had to market myself before, I am now receiving requests for interviews from high quality companies who want to start a conversation and see where it goes."

This is what you want for yourself. So get busy.

Just remember, job hunting is tough to do by yourself. Keep active by following these guidelines or you'll slide backwards.

- Communicate at least weekly with your networks.
- Embrace the new technologies and tools that are available to you and keep current with your options.
- Set some goals for every day and week.
- Join our Linked Executive Career Search Network Group on LinkedIn to follow discussions on the chapters in the book and on executive job search in general.
- Join our growing community at www.devonjames.com and use our resource library for further help.

The best of luck to you

I use the word "bedlam" in the book and in our program, since it means "a situation of chaotic uproar, where confusion prevails." I can't remember a time in my career when I've seen a worse employment situation in the U.S., and my heart goes out to those in the throes of it.

My hope is that I have helped you move forward in some way – through motivation or discovery – so that you land on your feet in a positive situation where all of your assets are being utilized and amply rewarded.

EPILOGUE

The Devon James Executive Job Search Program

If you're interested in having a partner to do all of this with you, please feel free to contact us. With your input, we will build your profile, and get you connected, positioned, and visible.

And most importantly, you'll come out of the Program with a renewed sense of self, confident in your strengths and talents. *After all, the situation you're in is most likely not your choice or your fault.* These are crazy times for us all.

More about the Devon James Executive Job Search Program can be found here: www.devonjames.com.

- access our client resource library
- join our LinkedIn Group
- register for one of our webinars
- sign up for a local seminar
- find out more about InterviewStudio
- see more detail about the full Executive Program

One of the networking resources we offer is a LinkedIn Group for executive job seekers. You are welcome to join us here.

Linked Executive Career Search Network

Any executive or recruiter can join the LinkedIn Group that we host called: Linked Executive Career Search Network. It's free. Your membership will let you see job search discussions, job postings, and other members of the Group that you can tap to trade information. Members include other executive job seekers, Employers, Career Coaches, and search professionals. Just go to www.Linkedin.com and search for this title (Linked Executive Career Search Network) under the Groups tab and join the group.

Index

ABOUT THE AUTHOR

Colleen Aylward has worked with senior managers on both sides of the hiring table in dozens of companies on the west coast for over 20 years. Articles about her forward-thinking and unabashed counsel for employers and job seekers can be found in Fast Company Magazine, Wall Street Journal, Washington CEO, SmartMoney, and in many employment blogs. One of the first to embrace video technology for employment purposes, she developed her InterviewStudio "Total Candidate Profile" in 2005 -- a comprehensive online aggregate of a candidate for use in presenting and screening executives for better match and shorter hiring cycles. Ms. Aylward lives in the Seattle area and is available for speaking engagements and individual or group consulting regarding creative recruiting strategies for employers and job search strategies for executives.

Made in the USA
Lexington, KY
12 August 2014